Soul Truth

BIANCA CARUANA

Dear Bea,

Thank you for your support.

Here's to more adventures.

With Love

Bianca

May all beings be free

Prologue

A mid-afternoon winter sun shone through the stained-glass windows of my studio apartment in a quiet backstreet of Sliema, Malta. It's important to me that the places I stay have an abundance of natural light. I love the sunshine on my face. I love watching tiny dust particles dance in the rays to the melodies of my daydreams.

My blog was turning seven that year. 10 November. I'll never forget the date. It was the day I left it all behind in exchange for a one-way ticket to Malaysia. It was the day I left him – my soul mate. I stood at the crossroads that year. What lay before me was the easy road, the hard road and the road of truth. Depending on my perception, all of those roads were to be trodden. Life is, after all, a medley: a choose-your-own-adventure storybook with the result of emotion. I was here to feel it all, and to listen to the subtle whispers that led me to where it was I ought to be going. Standing at that footbridge, looking forward to a future I had not met yet, a future without him, I had to trust. I just had to. If we don't trust, if we hold on too tightly, can we ever be free?

I suppose one advantage of letting go is that we open up the opportunity to become. Because we don't stay the same. For good reasons. If we didn't change, we would never grow. If we didn't grow, we would never know how limitless we are. Did that make the crossroads any less of a daunting vantage point? Hardly. But we could either flow like the unconfined waters of a river, or let the pressure bank up so high it flooded our internal plains.

I'd let go of a lot that year: a successful, albeit depleting, fourteen-year career, a decent eight-month attempt at a university degree, and a lifetime of adhering to other people's expectations of me. People pleasing is easier to let go of than our love stories. Those loves that fill our bodies with all the stars in the Milky Way, and we radiate light so far away that tiny specs of breathing skin sit and watch us in awe. This is a story about love – about all the manifestations of love. It is a story about finding love. About letting go of love. About falling in love and ultimately, remembering that we are love. I knew a time would come to share this story. It came to me in a dream once, many years ago, but the story had yet to unfold.

My eyes squinted at the sun. The light fluttered between my eyelashes. I'd found a moment of stillness – a mirage in chaos. If I'd learned anything about stillness in all those years, it was that it was the place we can feel the most, the place we can hear the most.

A gentle silence engulfed me that afternoon in Sliema. In that silence, I heard seven words as clear as the morning chimes of church bells: "It's time to write your book, Bianca."

Chapter 1 - The river

I'd never seen so many stars in the night sky. Millions of shimmering specks so delicately placed up there, staring down at me, transfixing me with wonder. The stars were only so mightily visible that night due to our location, somewhere downstream of the Kinabatangan River in Malaysia's Borneo. Far away from any light pollution. A place where nature exhibits its truest form.

Our guide, Eric, prompted us to keep silent as the motorised riverboat came to a quiet halt near the riverside mangroves.

"Look over there," he said.

My gaze followed his hands as he pointed to the mangroves in front of us. My eyes adjusted into focus amidst a black night and what I saw was a kind of mosaic, glistening synchronously in the dark.

"See the fireflies?" he said. "They are awakening."

Like a thousand tiny lighthouses, the fireflies put on a performance of bioluminescence to the philharmonic songs of cicadas in the nearby distance. It brought me into a deep state of presence. It was as though I was the only person watching that magnificent show. Wherever I seemed to look in those fleeting moments, I was filled with awe. I could feel the world inside of me.

It was a stark contrast to the week prior when I had been sitting at my desk beneath the brightness of harsh white tube lights, staring at the grey cubicle walls of my office, feeling enclosed by expectations, deadlines and detachment. I was stressed and anxious, with an increasing list of things to do and not enough time to do them. It had been a demanding year and it was only April. While, on the surface, I was happy about the promotion I'd been given and the recognition that came with it, I couldn't help but feel conflicted. As if, perhaps, I was heading down the path of someone else's dream, a path not paved for my feet to tread. Between that and the break-up, my mind was uneasy.

I'd always been clear I wasn't ready to settle down or even think about having children. I was only twenty-six. I'd barely shaken off the remnants of a self-deprecating puberty, years of living in accordance with the approval of others. I could feel myself beginning to cast off society's expectations of the woman I was like a diamond python shedding its skin. I inherently felt the typical boy-meets-girl-falls-in-love-marries-girl screenplay wasn't on the cards for me at that age. I was a well-educated, driven, ambitious woman who – thanks to the lineage of resolute women before me who traversed their way through the trenches of a patriarchal society – was able to grow up in a community where I had choices. I could choose any way I wanted to live my life and I could choose not to conform to any kind of societal norms. So, when he revealed to me, almost twelve months into our relationship, that he wanted to be married with children by the age of thirty, it came as quite a shock. Despite my wanting that for him and being open about not being able to give that to him, letting go caused a minor rift in our worlds.

The unsteadiness brought about by sudden changes in life can put anyone off course, no matter the dynamics of what led to that change. The decision to end a relationship is especially difficult. One moment a person is a significant part of your life and the next they are gone, vanished, a chapter ripped out of a book once read. And there is always a wound, even if not visible to the outside world. The challenge is to find the means necessary to sew your wound back together, take those lessons you've learned and continue on your journey to where it is you ought to be going. If you don't know where that is, ask for directions.

An impromptu journey to Borneo and Cambodia was the respite I needed to break away from my disordered life, even if only temporarily. For me back then, the transaction made for some breathing space in the forests was a fifty-hour work week, forty-eight weeks of the year. And I made that transaction, year after year, feeling as though that was the price I had to pay for my pleasure.

I ventured to the Malaysian side of the island of Borneo with a friend who was as curious about the world as I was. We'd bonded over our dreams to see the wonders of this earth, specifically places in vast contrast to the city we'd both grown up in: Sydney, Australia. Borneo piqued our interest, not only for its rich biodiversity but because we wanted to learn about the conservation efforts happening in the region. At the time, Borneo had lost almost fifty percent of its forests to deforestation – a devastating, capitalistic move to make way for the expansion of palm oil and pulpwood plantations, leading to the production of the same palm oil found in our own household goods such as ice creams, toothpaste, peanut butter … the list goes on. How unknowingly we are connected to the destruction of a natural world that keeps us alive, I pondered.

During that week in Borneo, I learned about the conservation efforts protecting sea turtles and orang-utans and visited one of the many protected wildlife sanctuaries we had been so inquisitive about: the lower Kinabatangan River Wildlife Sanctuary. The river is a stretch of 560 kilometres that connects the Sulu Sea to the mountains of Sabah, making it the second-longest river in Malaysia. Only a few small villages inhabit that part of the world, with a minimum population of around two hundred people per village. It was fascinating to witness a place where flora and fauna outnumbered humans, not the other way around.

As the afternoon fell that day on the Kinabatangan River, the temperature cooled behind a torrid, sultry day and many of the forest's inhabitants arrived at the water's edge for a refreshing drink. It allowed for some great wildlife spotting in that unspoiled wilderness: a place where the wild Bornean elephants roamed, proboscis monkeys jumped from tree-top to tree-top, crocodiles laid still under the mangroves, the solitary orang-utans made their nests, and the kingfishers and hornbills watched over the forest with the best views of all.

That evening, the sun set over the figured silhouettes of ficus trees, and the sky painted colours of purple and pink as the sounds of cicadas hushed the river's voice. An obsidian night greeted us and the only lights to be seen were from the fireflies taking refuge in the crannies of the bark, and the infinite stars that lit the night sky. I tuned in deeper to the cicada orchestra. My gaze drifted away from dancing fireflies and back up to the expansive canvas of stars above. I'd lost track of time for a moment and entered a state of deep reflection. *If I made a wish right now, if I sent out a magical intention to this vast universe, what would become of it?*

I hadn't asked for anything in quite some time. Life was, for the most part, pretty wonderful. I had the quintessential dream job, I had food on the table, a roof over my head, supportive friends and family. Yet, if I reflected deeper, on an innate plane, something felt unaligned. I felt an obstruction in the flow of my internal river. As though a part of my soul was stuck, banked up against a fallen trunk, seeking to flow down a different channel.

I closed my eyes to feel more. To feel the sounds of the forest, to tune in to the energy of that enchanting moment. *If there were ever a time to make a wish, it would be here, now, beneath this sea of stars, in this tranquil space away from the chaos of my other world.*

And so, there in the silent womb of the river, I asked for something – something that would change the course of my life and guide my soul in the direction it ought to be going.

Chapter 2 - In just one moment

The alarm sounded at five in the morning. Barely able to see in the pre-dawn darkness, I reached over to hit the snooze button but tactically decided against it and turned off the alarm instead. Squinty-eyed, I pulled the beige quilt off my body and sat up for a brief moment. Dazed by the regular dreams that inhabited my subconscious every evening, I reluctantly found the energy to get out of the warm bed and begin my mediocre dress routine for the day ahead.

For a woman who worked in a corporate setting, I had quite an unsatisfactory level of bother for my appearance. I much preferred an extra ten minutes of sleep to applying a full face of makeup, styling my hair and selecting a modish outfit. Since receiving the promotion, I had gathered a few relatively ordinary ensembles that made me look mildly professional and, perhaps, one or two smarter looks for when I had to take part in important meetings. Otherwise, my wardrobe was largely made up of thrift buys from the local flea market and some hand-me-downs from my two younger sisters. I was adamant my morning routine should last no greater than eighteen minutes from the moment I opened my eyes to getting in the car and driving the monotonous forty-eight minutes to the office.

Waking up at five in the morning was something I was very used to. I had, for many years, worked in the fruit and vegetable department of one of Australia's largest supermarkets. First, as a shop assistant, where my roles and responsibilities were to keep the shelves full and the produce tidy – something that had to be achieved in the early hours of the morning before the shoppers arrived. Then, as a quality control officer where my role was to make sure the fruit and vegetables were of a quality standard that met the store's approval and to not send any rotten produce onto the delivery truck to make its way onto some poor sod's dinner plate, only for them to make a complaint and sue the company for food poisoning. Then, as an assistant buyer where my role was to manage the inventory and ensure that each and every store in Australia had the correct number of boxes of fruit and vegetables daily, so they did not run out each evening and so no customer would have to go a day without their morning smoothie. And lastly, the cream-of-the-crop job title as a national buyer where my roles and responsibilities were much more senior. Before I knew it, or rather thirteen years later, I had climbed the corporate ladder to success. I had made it to the top. I had finally reached the career achievement I had been striving for all those years, or so I thought.

What is it about making it "to the top" that seems so alluring to us humans? Less people to tell us what to do? More autonomy? For me, it seemed the higher I climbed that corporate ladder, the more challenges I faced. Some days in the latter years of my career when I held a senior position, I dreamed of landing on a snake and sliding right back down to the bottom of that professional game of snakes and ladders, to a place with fewer responsibilities. I could be a cabinet lady, just like my old colleague, Marie. She worked four shifts a week. Clocked on at six am and clocked off at eleven am. On the dot. No deadlines. No spreadsheets. Just making sure the buk choy was filled and the oak green lettuce wasn't wilting. But I'd mostly landed on ladders in my career. It did come with its perks though. Like annual holidays, the latest tech products and enough disposable income to feed the capitalistic economy I existed in.

It was a chilly Friday morning in mid-July. I arrived at the office and drove down to level two of the underground car park to secure my usual car space before the building filled with vehicles. The head office I worked in was a huge glass-paned building that took up almost half the suburb it occupied. There was space for the thousands of cars of the thousands of employees who powered that multibillion-dollar machine. It took at least ten minutes to get from the car park up the many levels and down the many hallways to reach my office cubicle.

"Morning!" I heard Dave, one of my co-workers, greet me as I walked towards the building entrance.

"Good morning," I replied.

"You look tired. Big night?" he asked.

"TGIF," I replied flippantly, with a smirk.

Wasn't it mildly impolite to tell someone they looked tired at six in the morning? Of course, I was tired, Dave. I'd woken up at five for the past six days and had already worked forty-five hours that week. I wasn't about to tell Dave that though.

That Friday was a Friday like any other: manage all the orders, schedule calls with some of the produce growers, make sure the team knew what needed to be done over the weekend. At around midday, my phone vibrated on the desk beside my keyboard and the screen lit up with a message notification. It was my old friend Matt.

The message read, "What are you up to tonight? I'm having a birthday gathering at mine and then we're going clubbing. You're welcome to join. ~ Matt."

My first thoughts were of a reluctant kind. I was exhausted from a long week in the office and inundated with tasks and responsibilities. It was almost the weekend though, and I did have a rare weekend off which only occurred every three weeks (one of the disadvantages of working in retail). Without thinking too much about it, I put my phone away in my jacket pocket and continued on with my pressing work. By the end of the day, I had almost forgotten about the message.

Just before I turned the ignition in my car to leave the office building for the day, my phone lit up again.

"We're meeting at mine at seven. Hope to see you there. ~ Matt."

This time, my reluctance had evolved into more of an intrigue. After all, it was Matt's birthday and I hated to miss my friends' birthdays. As the weight of the week lifted off me and I left the mental snippets of spreadsheets and SAP screens back inside that dour premises, a part of me felt excited to meet some new people. After my recent trips to Borneo and Cambodia, connecting with other travellers and welcoming thrilling experiences, I felt a slight sense of nostalgia for that. There was something about being in a room full of people you'd met for the first time, an exhilarating sense of anticipation. It was a reminder that in just one moment your life could change.

That evening, I rode Sydney's rather efficient public transport system and arrived at Matt's apartment in the eastern suburb of Kensington. The mid-winter evening brought early dusk and a half-moon illuminated above us, peering behind scattered clouds. I pressed number 5 and waited for the door to make a buzzing sound. As I ascended two flights of stairs, a faint feeling of nervousness washed over me. *Or was it excitement?* I couldn't tell. The apartment door was ajar and so I let myself in, removing my black, short-heeled ankle books and placing them on the shoe rack among the others.

"Hello," I said, listening to the sound of chatter coming from the living room.

Matt glanced at me from down the hallway. He was already walking in my direction. I hadn't seen those warm brown eyes and those rosy cheeks in a long time. He felt familiar.

"Hi Bee!" he said as he walked closer to me and embraced me in a tight hug. "It's so great to see you. Thanks for coming."

"Happy birthday!" I said as I hugged him back.

Matt escorted me into the living room where other guests stood, engaged in their own conversations.

"Everyone, this is Bianca," he signalled over the chatter. He turned his gaze toward me. "I think you've met some people here, but there may be some new faces."

The crowd turned to me, smiled, acknowledged my presence and continued on with their discussions, beers in hand.

"Let me get you a drink," Matt said as he walked into the kitchen.

I stood beside the white four-person dining table in the L-shaped kitchen of the apartment while he opened the fridge. In the connecting lounge room, I could hear vague snippets of conversation. I eyed the room and listened to the discussions, calculating where and when to add my presence. While scanning the crowd, I noticed a tall, dark-haired man speaking to Matt. He was someone I had not met, a face not so familiar. He stood out to me though, as if everything around him blurred and we were the only two people in the room. He held himself with confidence and his laugh eclipsed all others. He looked to be in his mid-to-late twenties, handsome, with a distinct mallen streak in his hair. He was wearing black denim jeans, a grey leather jacket and some white Nike kicks, the ones with the black tick on either side of each shoe. He caught my gaze and our eyes connected for a moment. He briefly smiled at me as if to acknowledge my presence, but not long enough to assume it was flirtatious. I smiled back, but then shyly looked away and continued to stand comfortably by Matt, following him around like a little sister on her first day of school.

"Let's head out. I'll round up the troops," Matt said, as the party continued.

We walked towards the front door. In my direction was the man who'd caught my gaze earlier on. Our eyes met once again, this time I was close enough to notice their livid blue colour.

"I don't think we've met, I'm Bianca," I said as I reached out my hand to invite a handshake.

"I'm Dean. Nice to meet you," he responded.

We followed the group through the hallway, down the two flights of stairs and out to the curb side to hail a taxi headed for Sydney's infamous Oxford Street – an animated spot housing the majority of Sydney's late-night venues. A night on Oxford Street meant a surety for a party. And it certainly was.

I danced so much that evening. The club atmosphere was like a 1970s disco with multicoloured strobe lights peering through the crowds and vapour in the air from the DJ's smoke machine. It had been a while since I had gone clubbing like that. I had forgotten how infectious the energy of a room full of hundreds of dancing bodies could be – a synchronous frequency of liberation.

As night turned to morning and our blood turned to alcohol, we were lost in the music. The more I let go of my inhibitions and allowed my body to move along to the rhythm of the beats, the further away I became from those grey walls I had spent the day enclosed in. By roughly three in the morning, there were only four of our group left at the club.

"Let's head back for a nightcap," Matt signalled to us over the music.

I followed him, weaving through the dwindling crowd towards the exit. None of us was ready to sleep, consumed by the energy of an ecstatic evening.

Back at Matt's house, we chatted away about life and such things until the early hours of the morning. By that time, Matt had pulled a blow-up mattress into the living room and dozed off under the blankets while Dean and I sat on the couch, exchanging tales of adventures abroad and a twenties well lived. He was funny. At times he made me laugh so much that my cheeks hurt. I was surprised our contagious laughter didn't wake Matt, asleep just metres away.

We spoke more in those early hours of the morning than we had at all throughout the night. There was no flirting of any kind. But as we sat there next to each other that evening in mid-July, amidst a silent, sleeping room, laughing and joking and edging closer and closer to one another on that couch, a love kindled. We didn't know it at the time. We were just two, young wandering souls existing in a turbulent world who had somehow found our way into each other's company on that winter evening, as the continent beneath us rotated towards the sun.

Dean was in the middle of telling me a story about one debaucherously eventful evening when he met one of the members of the band, MGMT, in a bar in Houston, Texas. I listened to him attentively, but the more he spoke, the longer my gaze fixated on him and all I could think about was how beautiful he looked. His soft olive-toned skin, those livid blue eyes. He was gentle yet exuberant, confident yet unassuming. His energy captivated me like the calming waves of an ocean.

He was mid-sentence when my captivation transformed into action and, in a rather brave, sudden expression of endearment, I leaned over and placed my lips on his for just a short second, and then pulled back nervously. I felt like a young girl, mustering up the courage to bravely kiss her crush for the first time.

Dean looked at me with surprise. His eyes were as wide as I ever saw them. His facial expression signified the kiss was unanticipated and caught him unaware, but then he smiled at me with the most adoring, affiliative smile, placed his soft fingers on my cheek, and kissed me back.

As the first morning light hit the horizon, I curled up into the crevice that was him, closed my eyes and drifted off to sleep. That was the day my life changed forever.

Chapter 3 - A love blooming

Dean's and my relationship bloomed like a flower in spring. We would speak on the phone for hours. I think our record was twelve intermittent hours on the phone one weekend I came down with a terrible flu and couldn't leave the house. His presence created a space where I felt completely safe, a space where I showed up with a kind of authenticity I never knew I was capable of.

Young love does that to us. In our fiercely besotted states, we show up in our truest form, forgetting to put up the facades we so commonly live behind. In those seemingly flawless periods of utmost requited adoration, we can feel invincible, adored like kings and queens simply for existing. *Have you ever felt more beautiful than when you are truly loved for the first time by someone who was once a stranger?* In those moments of rawness, we are seen as we are because we show who we are. Yet, outside of love, we don't often allow others to see us wholly, despite deeply desiring to be seen in our wholeness. Outside of love, we can put up walls, wear masks, tell altered narratives. We can tend to hide the deepest parts of ourselves away from the people in our lives. Perhaps it is fear that leads us to show up inauthentically: fear of being judged, of hurting someone, of being hurt, of facing emotions that have been tucked away so deeply we've lost complete sight of them. But when young love is blooming, fear is defaced. And we had a fearless love, Dean and me. We quickly became a reflection of each other's wholeness.

Dean and I came from similar backgrounds. We grew up in the same suburbs in Sydney's south-east. There was less than a year's difference in our ages. He was an '85 baby, I was '86. This meant we shared the same nostalgia for the nineties and noughties. We got each other's references. We were able to clearly visualise when the other told a story about their life, their past. We both collected Pokémon cards as children. We both vividly remembered where we were on 9/11 when the Twin Towers catastrophe aired on every television station in the country. We grew up listening to the same hip-hop artists. We even frequented the same hangouts in our teens and twenties.

"I bet our paths crossed when we were younger," I would say to him. "I wish I had a time machine to go back and see when and where I saw you for the first time. Imagine if we danced at Carmen's Nightclub back in its heyday."

"I would have been hanging with the boys in a corner somewhere, not taking notice of anything except the rhythm of the music," he replied.

He was probably right. Dean was not like other boys. He wasn't the type to approach women or gawk over pretty girls in the club. He was loyal to his friends and comfortable on his own, in his own world. He had a mysterious, solitary side, and I liked that about him. It meant he wasn't intimidated by my fierce independence. Even that morning after we kissed for the first time, I was the one who signalled him to put his number in my phone. If I hadn't done so, he may have walked out of that room, and I would have never seen him again. But I had no qualms about asking a guy to put his number in my phone. I never complied with any gender stereotypes like that. If I saw something I liked, I would go for it.

The two of us became very close, very quickly. Our conversations were never surface level. He entertained my deep thoughts with attentive ears and reciprocated answers. He always seemed to be interested in the things I had to say, no matter how otherworldly. My mind tended to get lost in chambers of existential theories and the meanings of reality. I was a dreamer at heart. I saw symbols, metaphors and hidden messaging embedded in all aspects of life, and it felt natural to communicate it so, when I felt safe enough to express that side of myself. Dean, on the other hand, was a realist. He was pragmatic and relished life's certainties. Although we differed in that sense, we complemented each other. He was my roots, and I was his wings. His pragmatism brought me back down to earth on days I'd wander far beyond the end of the rainbow.

"Would you like to try some of my meal?" I prompted him at dinner that evening.

"No thank you," he responded politely.

I noticed Dean would rarely take me up on the offer to share my meal while eating his. He ate his meals like he conducted his business, with structure, precision and routine. To the contrary, I would eat my meals concomitantly, almost always attempting to reach my fork over into his dish and explore the contents of his plate. I relished life's variety and enjoyed experiencing the blend of flavours brought about by creating weird concoctions of my own meals. Evidently, one could tell a lot about a person by the way they ate.

That same evening while sipping on some imported sangiovese chianti and talking about where we saw ourselves in ten years' time, I asked Dean to play a game with me.

"Let's think of ten things we want to do in the next ten years," I said with inordinate excitement.

"Hmm, I'll have to have a good think about that one," he responded.

I hastily leapt off the couch to find some pieces of paper.

"We'll write them down," I said. "When you write things down on paper with pure intentions, you're making a pact with the universe that you'll get them done."

17

We sat in silence, full of inspiration, the curious cogs in our minds accessing our deepest dreams and desires.

"Let me see yours?" I impatiently peeked over his shoulder to see his handwritten notes on the crinkled piece of paper I had ripped from a nearby notebook.

"OK, I'll share them with you," he said.

He looked down at his words and commenced reading his list to me like a student presenting an essay in a classroom, "Study philosophy. Participate in an amateur boxing match. Forge a sword. Learn Italian. See the Northern Lights. Go to Tibet. See the Eiffel Tower..."

"I love Paris!" I interrupted him as he spoke. "It's one of my favourite cities in the world."

"What do you have on your list?" he asked me.

I looked down at my piece of paper and examined what I had written. "Learn to play the piano. Backpack through South America. Write a book. Learn a language. Visit Nepal. Share someone's story. Be in love in Europe ..."

"Why only Europe?" Dean asked.

"Because ... it's romantic," I replied with an indicative smile.

"Well, Europe is not the only romantic place in the world," he responded. "This can be romantic."

Dean stood up and then grabbed my hand to lift me up from the cross-legged position I was sitting in on the floor of his studio apartment. I looked at him with curious eyes.

"Wait for a second," he said as he selected a song from Spotify on his phone.

The white noise that surrounded us was soon interrupted by the distinct saxophone beats to Louis Armstrong's 'La Vie en Rose,' resounding through the room. As the smile on my face grew wider, I walked up to him, put my hands around his shoulders and looked into his eyes with immense adoration. Our bodies drifted side to side along with the lyrics,

Hold me close and hold me fast
The magic spell you cast
This is la vie en rose ...

"Europe can be here tonight," he said.

We were both dreamers at that moment. Together we extended past the limits of our conscious minds and into a world of endless possibilities. I loved how we'd go on profound journeys of self-reflection like that, unveiling intricate pieces of ourselves and learning more about each other as each day went by. Those types of conversations, like the one in pretend-Paris that evening, not only made me see him more clearly but I started to see myself clearer. It was as if he was my magic mirror, a chance to examine my reflection and unveil who I was in my truest form.

It was surprising that, for both of us, our goals didn't consist of attaining material belongings or acquiring monetary wealth. Neither of us had suggested in the next ten years we'd desire a family or a four-bedroom home with a white picket fence. There was no pressure to settle down or be married by the age of thirty. Our goals were centred around adventure and personal growth, the acquisition of knowledge, and a longing to progress outside of our comfort zones.

Yet, as we stood there dancing and dreaming that night, we were dancing deep inside a cocoon of comfort we had co-created.

Chapter 4 - The catalyst

The next morning, I woke up at an early 5:15 am. It was late January and so daylight savings meant the mornings were darker than usual. I had spent the night at Dean's place which meant the drive to the office was roughly fourteen minutes shorter, so I took pleasure in the extra sleep. I was feeling slightly fatigued. Partly due to the chianti and partly due to the fact I was inundated with responsibilities at the office. I was good at my job, but I was also a high achiever, which was great for my output but not so great for my well-being.

Work–life balance was a concept only beginning to surface in the corporate setting. It was the days before remote work and Zoom calls in our pyjama bottoms. Before companies began acknowledging mental health awareness and implementing sensible compliance, especially big corporations who tended to be the last ones adopting the widespread practice. I recall less than two conversations in my corporate career where employee mental well-being was vaguely touched upon, but it was more of a box-ticker statement along the lines of "talk to your manager if you are experiencing any 'issues'" rather than a serious matter openly discussed. Showing any sign of mental struggle in the workforce was considered a weakness for a person in a senior position like mine. And it didn't help that I was one of the few women in leadership, supervised by a lengthy hierarchy of ostentatious and mildly priggish males.

I was in a position that required me to wear many hats. I would start my day with intense and timely administration tasks. It was absolutely crucial that all orders be finalised by eight am. My team and I were essentially responsible for procuring enough produce to feed the whole nation of Australia, and I was responsible for maintaining fair and equitable relationships with a number of vendors and produce growers who facilitated that procurement.

It was one of those let-me-find-an-hour-in-my-day-in-two-weeks-time-to-book-a-meeting kind of roles. I was busy, all the time. But it became normal for me. I was on constant autopilot, a scratched record so far in the depths of regime and schedule that I may as well have been a computer program coded in such a way to ensure precise and maximum outcome.

"Your one pm has arrived. They're waiting in the foyer," said the voice on the other side of the phone.

I took a quick sip of water from the glass beside my keyboard and grabbed the relevant folder on my desk.

As I walked through the narrow maze of office cubicles, I met the direction of my manager who was also attending the meeting.

"Do you have everything you need?" he asked.

"Yes. I've got the figures and have some suggestions on where we can improve," I replied.

We walked together down the hallway and to the main foyer to meet our guests. After greeting them, we headed down to Quarter B which housed the larger meeting rooms. We were meeting with two leaders and two other members of one of the company's largest growers' corporations. I knew one of them well enough to feel slightly less awkward and less likely to put on the fake professional facade I frequently portrayed in those types of interactions. The energy in those meetings was always so rigid. It was as if we were playing roles as actors in a drama screenplay. We all had hidden agendas disguised behind a forced charm in order to maintain civility, but mostly to obtain an upper hand. There always firm negotiations to minimise confrontation, and discussions requiring assertiveness and ruthlessness. I remembered something my former manager had told me before I was promoted to this position: "You'll have to be ruthless in this role to get ahead, Bianca."

Ruthlessness wasn't exactly my forte, nor did it fit my character in any way. I had a gentle nature. I was emotional, nurturing, intuitive and highly sensitive. I was the shy one in school. The feedback on my report cards year after year was almost identical. They would read: "Bianca is a fine student, but she should participate more in class discussions." I never put my hand up in class. I didn't want attention drawn to me, and if it was, it resulted in feelings of overwhelm. I suppose it was a classical characteristic of an introverted nature, but although I was an introvert, I was able to develop strong and long-lasting relationships with certain people. I suppose in some ways I was an extroverted introvert. Once I felt comfortable enough with certain people, I was able to completely let them in to read the pages of my world and I no longer felt like hiding parts of myself. I carried this reserved nature into my adult life, navigating an existence in a society that rewarded more outgoing personality traits and discouraged individuality.

The standard expectation for life where I grew up went something along the lines of: go to school, go to university, get the job, earn the money, get the car, get the house, start the family and so on. When I was just sixteen years old, I received a toy model Bburago Ferrari for my birthday, along with a card that read: "Work hard enough and you'll be able to buy the real one someday." I didn't recall ever wishing to amount to life with a Ferrari, but I appreciated the sentiment, nonetheless.

My family wanted me to be successful, as most families want for their loved ones, but at the time, their vision of success was very different to mine. In fact, I had never really thought to define what success meant to me. No one had ever asked me the question, "What does success mean to you?" You the individual, not you the collective. So, I had never really reflected on success. Was it obtaining a Ferrari? Was it making sure the oak green lettuce wasn't wilting? Was it sitting under the glaring, unflattering white light of a meeting room negotiating the cutting of costs so a multibillion-dollar enterprise could fatten its bottom line?

"What are your thoughts, Bianca?" I heard a voice ask. It startled me out of a daydream.

In contrast with the ghost white walls, the bright lights had exacerbated my headache and I was feeling mildly uncomfortable. I opened my mouth and began to string a sentence together.

"After looking through the figures I'd like to specifically discuss ..."

I paused for a moment. My thoughts were muddled. It was as if my mind was a recently shaken snow globe. I reached for the folder on the table in front of me and noticed my palms had begun to perspire. As I turned to find the correct page in the folder, I saw my fingers trembling, noticeably. At that moment, I completely lost my thoughts. It was like my body was in that chair, but I was somewhere else. My senses were heightened, but I was unable to function normally.

"Excuse me, I am feeling slightly unwell. I'm going to get some air." I stood abruptly from my chair, knocking it over in the process, and headed to the doorway. I needed out. I needed to be anywhere but there. My manager followed me outside of the room.

"Are you OK?" he asked.

"I ... I don't think so," I responded.

"I'll take over from here, we've almost finished anyway," he assured me.

As I walked up the stairs to the floor where my office cubicle was, I took a detour to the women's restroom. I was feeling extremely overwhelmed and dazed. I opened the door to a cubicle, placed the toilet seat down and sat there for a moment to process what had happened. Tears began streaming down my cheeks as I sat there alone, shaken by the event that had transpired.

I'm not OK, said the voice in my head. *What am I doing here? This isn't who I am. I'm so embarrassed. I want to be anywhere but here.* A tsunami of thoughts engulfed me. My first instinct was to reach for the phone in my pocket and call Dean.

It rang out on the first try. It was the middle of the day and Dean would have been working at his desk or likely in a meeting. He was in a senior position in his career. He managed a team of engineers for a building services consultancy firm in Sydney's north and was very fond of his job. His professional career took off in his early twenties as he became one of the first subject-matter experts on building information modelling, the foundation of digital transformation in the architecture, engineering and construction industries. When it came to his sprouting career, he would always say that he was just in the right place at the right time, but the truth was, he was incredibly intelligent, driven and determined. Once he set himself a goal, he would do whatever it took to accomplish it.

On the second attempt, I heard Dean's comforting voice on the other end of the line.

"Hey, I'm just at work. Is everything OK?" he asked.

"Not really," I answered with a gasping voice. "I think I just had an anxiety attack at work."

"Wait a few seconds. I am going to leave my desk so I can talk to you," he responded.

He could sense it was a serious matter. Throughout our relationship, we were always there for one another, especially in times of trouble.

Dean was extremely loyal and the type of person who would show up for the people he loved. I saw him exhibit this trait not only in our own relationship, but with his friends and family as well. He wanted to see people happy. Perhaps it derived from his family lineage of circus performers, entertaining and bringing joy to the people of Australia for over eight generations. Dean would tell me stories about how his grandfather and grandmother performed shows across regional Australia and how they would travel from city to city with their imaginative ensemble, living a life less ordinary. His grandfather, Les, used to perform acrobatics on horseback. His grandmother spun on aerial ropes, held only by her teeth. When Dean was younger, his father Glen used to spin the tale that the scar he obtained beneath his right jawline was from a lion that had gotten loose from an enclosure one day and crept into his tent when he was a baby. Dean believed that fable until he was twelve years old.

"What happened? Are you OK?" Dean's voice instantly started to soothe my weathered self.

"I don't know. I just became so overwhelmed. I'm so exhausted." I replied.

"Why don't you leave work now and I can try and get out early and meet you at my apartment? We can talk about everything," he responded with a sympathetic tone.

I left work early that day, trying to hide the fact I had been weeping uncontrollably in the women's restroom. I didn't want to bring any attention to myself. I couldn't bring myself to try and explain to anyone what was going on. It wasn't just the panic attack. I had been feeling so off-centre. Something had shifted in me since returning from my time abroad. I was witnessing my life from an alternate vantage point, realising how this job was consuming me from the outside in. *Was this the sign I asked for months beforehand that starry night in Borneo? Was my body speaking to me?* Just like the pressure that builds up when water is unable to flow freely, so does the force of our own emotions. I had been running on autopilot for so long, engaging in a continuous cycle of repetition and routine. I hadn't been able to see the forest through the trees of my own wellbeing. If my body was calling out to me, it was saying one thing... Stop.

Chapter 5 - Descending the corporate ladder

I sat on the intricately patterned Persian rug in the living room of Dean's apartment on the 20th floor and looked out the balcony door over Sydney's vast skyline. The sun was setting over the horizon and the coloured patchwork of clouds in the twilight offered me respite. My eyes were heavy from the constant flow of tears triggered by a release of intense emotion, an indication of the day that was and possibly the months that were. I had at least made my way into a seated position as opposed to my former sobbing foetal position. Perhaps a grown adult finding their way into a foetal position on any kind of floor, longing for their mother's solace, is a cue for change; a testament to an opportunity for rebirth.

"I feel as though I'm not where I am supposed to be," I explained to Dean as he looked at me the way one would look at a hurt puppy.

I knew it would have been hard for him to see me in that state. Even his comical one-liners weren't enough to put an optimistic grin on my face, and he was almost always able to use his unique humour to evoke a smile.

"I've spent all these years climbing some ladder to success and I'm here. I have everything you're supposed to have, but there is an emptiness inside of me I can't explain," I continued.

"You've been quite unhappy in your job for a while," he said. "Maybe you should just quit. It's weighing on you."

I'd been thinking about leaving my job for many years. An instinctive part of me knew I was heading down a path not meant for me. I felt it in my heart, but the voices in my head would drown out the heart's messages like a loud concert playing over subdued words.

The voices were doubtful and fuelled by fear. *What would I do? What about my income? What about all the years I've spent to amount to this version of me? What will everyone think?*

People in my workplace rarely left the company. Another month, another work anniversary, another home brand cake in the breakout room to say thank you for the past fifteen years of service and then back to the computer screen. Between the forty-odd people in our team, the average number of years in service at the company was twelve. Not to say everyone was as unconvinced as I. For some, a secure job with generous wages meant they could provide decently for their families. They could spend the weekends assembling IKEA furniture, pruning the gardens, visiting the farmers' market and taking their children to the sports ground. They could fill their homes with fine decor, leather sofas, expressionist art pieces and various dining sets, one for casual engagements and one for formal evenings with acquaintances. They could take the yearly holiday, increase their retirement funds and drive the SUV. But as I grew older, as much as I thought those things would be important to me, they just weren't. So not only did the thought of quitting my job and my whole career make my stomach churn with nerves, it also made me feel as though I was the one fish swimming in the opposite direction to all the others – the one with spots and not stripes. The one heading into an ocean of the complete unknown.

"What would I even do if I quit? I've spent the past thirteen years working in this career. Who am I without this?" I continued to express my thoughts out loud.

"We'll figure it out," Dean responded. "Look how much experience you've gained. You're intelligent, you're ambitious. You can be anything you want to be."

I couldn't help but feel a sense of serendipity in his words. Only a few years prior to that emotional breakdown, I had started writing my first blog, coincidentally, or not coincidentally, titled *Be Where You*

Want To Be. During one of my first transformational journeys abroad to India, I felt inclined to journal about the experiences I had there, and that journaling re-ignited my spark for reflective writing. I'd never studied English literature but was always drawn to the written word. Writing was a way for me to express myself. It was a medium with relative obscurity and so I felt protected behind my written words. The paper was non-judgemental, the keyboard did not censor me. Or perhaps, I may rephrase: *I* did not feel judged by the paper. *I* did not feel censored by the keyboard.

I'd always had journals. They were either paperback notebooks filled with expressions about my latest crush who hardly knew I existed or rambling projections of the teenage angst I felt towards my parents at the time. Or, later on in my life, I'd use the notes application on my smartphone and fill it with maunderings about the way I saw the world, things I wished to say but didn't know how, and the occasional poem I'd write after an encounter that filled me with inspiration.

Throughout the last year of my corporate career, I'd spend the Saturday afternoons I was stuck in the office writing about travel and philanthropy. Once I ensured every store in Australia had enough button mushrooms to fill their cabinets for the day, I closed the SAP screens, opened my blog and painted the computer screens with the colours of my words. Perhaps the name of my first blog, *Be Where You Want To Be,* was a message from my soul, a message I had not yet honoured, stifled by my own self-doubt. *Who was I without that career? Who are we without the identities we attach to?*

When we are born, we are immediately given an identity. That identity consists of our name, our gender, our family, our nationality and so on. Those identities go on to define us, they define who we are. And as we grow, we add to those identities like pictures to a scrapbook. We add our education, our job, our relationships, our beliefs, and we become a finished puzzle – the embodiment of an accumulation of pieces of us. But what if one day we are no longer those pieces? Do we continue to stay a finished puzzle, or do we remove the pieces of our identity that no longer serve us, accept that, perhaps, we are an imperfect, unfinished puzzle, and then open up opportunities for transformation into something new? Just like the cycle of death and rebirth.

In the Buddhist faith, attachment is seen as one of the three *kleshas* (mental states that cloud the mind). If attachment arises, suffering occurs because we no longer accept the truth of our impermanent nature. Yet attachment is all around us. We are attached to many things, especially our own identities. I didn't realise it at the time, but I had subtly commenced the detachment of pieces of my identity that no longer fit in my perfectly imperfect puzzle.

When I started writing again, I was subconsciously beginning to shift my identity. I started to tap into creativity in me that had been repressed by a monotonous routine – those mechanical routines that keep us more focused on productivity and less focused on presence. Despite being completely unrelated to the work I was doing in my daily job, I sought education through courses and alternative studies. I took a course in web development and marketing. I took a short course in travel writing, where I vividly recall surprising myself with a local travel article I wrote about observing the migration of humpback whales off the cliffs of Cape Solander in Sydney's Kurnell. That article subsequently got picked up by a local newspaper and became my first ever published piece of writing. Although it was difficult to fit tasks like that into my busy schedule, they brought me joy and steadily helped to strip me away from the version of myself who sat unconvincingly in that office chair, day after day.

At times when I would daydream about a different life for myself, I would go down inspiration-seeking rabbit holes, looking for guidance and wisdom in anecdotal stories from people who had taken a leap of faith – who had found the courage to live their truth. Some of the most inspiring words I uncovered were one day, when I came across a snippet on YouTube from Jim Carrey's commencement speech to university students at MIU.

He encouragingly said, "I learned many great lessons from my father, not the least of which is that you can fail at what you don't want, so you might as well take a chance on doing what you love."

When I heard those words, I had an epiphany. I realised the emptiness I was feeling was because there was no love in my work. Not one part of my being felt even the most minuscule slice of passion for what I was doing. I was merely existing, floating aimlessly downstream, directionless, with no compass in my hands or in my heart. I could have continued floating down that river. I could have simply settled for my life at the time and convinced myself it was enough. But there was a voice in me. She was fierce and strong, and she was ever so graciously screaming out for me to listen to her.

It can oftentimes be difficult to hear our inner voice with all the chaos and noise we absorb from the outside world. It is said we can think up to 70,000 thoughts every day and 90 percent of those thoughts are the same as the day before. Our minds are a sponge to conditional thinking, ensnaring information from our past, present and future and creating illusions, or delusions, that often don't serve us. To hear what is really true, we must not only look to our minds but consult with the heart first and foremost. I believe there are many times we reach a fork in our road of life and have to listen deeply to understand which direction we should take. Sometimes, that decision is obvious. Other times, it requires a Sherlock Holmes-like internal investigation into who we are, and what it is we truly value.

"There is more for me in this existence, I can feel it," I explained to Dean. "I want to make a difference in the world. I truly do. I want to feel like I move through this world with purpose. I don't yet know what that looks like but I'm starting to know what it doesn't look like, and it doesn't look like this – this constant grind and a perpetual feeling of disconnectedness."

Although Dean was often my soundboard, and a good one at that, there were times I would unintentionally compare myself to him and his uncomplicated circumstances, influenced by his easy-going nature and ability to flow through life confidently, albeit haphazardly.

"Don't you ever feel like there is more to life?" I would ask with an expression resembling a child who had not yet learned to walk.

To which his response was almost always something modest like, "I'm happy to take life as it comes. I don't really need much."

A part of me was inspired by his ability to revere life's simplicities. He could contentedly power through any week, catch up with his mates on a Thursday night for a casual drink at the pub, watch reruns of *Frasier*, fit in a few personal training sessions at the gym, and that was enough for him. It would leave the non-inspired part of me pondering, in a pool of self-deprecation: *Why was it not enough for me?*

Despite catching myself mid-negative thought and revisiting a quote by Theodore Roosevelt that read "Comparison is the thief of joy," I still felt a sense of guilt for protesting against my perfectly adequate life. But I was so engulfed by lack and longing at the time, I couldn't find a fulfilling state of contentment. And the messages had been getting louder too. This wasn't the first time I had an inclination I was on the wrong path. Purpose had been increasingly nudging at me like a distant friend calling in to remind me they were there.

Throughout the earlier years of my life, I persistently felt a desire to help others. I remember the first year I received a stable weekly income, I was just a sprouting teenager scanning groceries at the local supermarket on the weekends (yes, the same supermarket I continued to work at for twelve more years). I took that well-earned paycheck to the shopping mall and, instead of spending the wages on some designer jeans and a new pair of trendy shoes, I walked up to a World

Vision pop-up stall and inquired about sponsoring a child from Uganda. Cavin was her name, a young girl from Kitgum in the country's north and only six years my junior. As a sponsor, my regular donations would provide economic relief for Cavin and her community, and over the course of the succeeding eleven years, Cavin and I stayed in contact sharing many letters and photographs as we grew from young girls into young women.

It wasn't until August 2013 that I visited Cavin for the first time. It was on the back of a whirlwind adventure across four countries in East Africa with nineteen other explorers, in a rickety bus we called Pumba. Back in Australia, I had enquired with World Vision about the opportunity to facilitate a meeting with Cavin in her home village of Kitgum, Uganda, and was elated when they advised me it was possible. Francis, my driver for the journey, and Robert, my sponsorship representative, arrived to pick me up from a hotel in the country's capital of Kampala. We then set off on the semi-long eight-hour drive north to Kitgum. The half-completed tarmac roads and lack of urban development were a reflection of almost two decades of ruinous conflict and civil unrest that had terrorised the districts of Gulu, Kitgum and Pader. The conflict all but completely destroyed northern Uganda's economic base. Only in 2008 were the last of the people in displacement camps returned to their villages, some never knowing what life was like outside the protective camps.

I had been in Africa for over three weeks. The vast savannah grasslands and sandy clay earth had become a familiar sight, prompting a faint nostalgia for the endless desert plains of the Australian outback. Despite heading to a region recently out of conflict, I didn't exhibit any feelings of fear but rather an enthusiasm and eagerness to meet the young woman who had played such a subtle, yet significant, role in my life.

This wasn't the first time I had been to parts of the world that were vastly different to my birthplace. Less than two years prior to my visit to Africa, I spent time in Rajasthan, India, taking in the sights of what the tourism industry called "The Golden Triangle" – a circuit that connected the national capital Delhi with surrounding cities, Agra and Jaipur. That experience humbled me and opened my eyes to the truth of our infinite world. I learned that we weren't just the places we came from – that there was an expansive spectrum of worlds within worlds on this magnificent planet Earth. That journey to India sparked something inside of me – a deep compassion, a remarkable feeling of worldliness and intrigue. And similar feelings arose that day in northern Uganda as the car pulled up to the small village where Cavin and her family resided.

In the nearby distance, I could hear the faint sound of a woman's voice becoming gradually louder. I looked in the rear-view mirror of the four-wheel drive and saw a woman following us, jubilantly waving her hands, clapping and singing as we drove into the centre of the village. The Ugandan woman was dressed in a long lemon-coloured gown with a bright cherry headscarf wrapped around her hair and what looked like a batik-printed multicoloured skirt around her waist. Her silhouette blended into a backdrop of clouded skies, clay-red soil, shrubs and shea nut trees. Following closely behind her was a small group of young children, pacing briskly to keep up. They had wide smiles on their curious faces, marvelling at the infrequent sight of foreigners entering their neighbourhood. As the car pulled to a stop in a clearing between two traditional huts, more of the villagers had come to greet us. Robert explained to me that the woman singing was engaging in a traditional custom with the purpose to notify the village that guests had arrived. He told me it was common practice for the community to put on a show of song and dance to commemorate the arrival of guests.

As I disembarked from the muddy, white, World Vision-branded ute, I came face to face with the beautiful young woman who had been part of my life for such a long time but whom I had never met. Until that day, I'd only ever seen Cavin in the photographs she sent. She was taller than I imagined. Her skin was soft like velvet. I remembered her as a child. She looked wiser now. I sensed womanhood had approached her faster than most. She gradually walked towards me and for a moment we stood eye to eye. Two women. Two dreamers. She put out her hand to invite a handshake that swiftly evolved into an embracing hug, as it felt natural to do so. It was a moment I had played out in my mind so many times and, as I held back tears of joy, the moment planted itself in my personal, cherished treasure chest of memories.

Robert directed us into one of the homes so we could become acquainted with Cavin and her family. Cavin's home was one of a dozen circular thatched-roof huts in the compound. It had a high-peak roof and was designed with a sleeping platform made from dried mud and cow dung. There was a platform for cooking, and carved shelves to hold jars of grain and other necessities. There was one small opening in the roof above the cooking station so the smoke from the fire stove could emit from the interior, and as a way for the light to enter. There was no electricity, nor running water. The pit latrines were located in a separate area, away from the homes, and the water was fetched daily from a local stream. It was common to find clusters of huts together for extended families who utilised the natural resources surrounding them. The societal structures in that part of the world held more emphasis on the community nucleus. It wasn't uncommon for a whole family to live beneath those thatched roofs. It reminded me how long I'd been a part of a deeply individualistic societal structure. One where we'd become perceptibly segregated from one another, both in external space and internal connection.

I sat near the hut opening, along with Robert, Cavin, her father and her aunt. Occasionally, children from the village would peek their inquisitive faces through the door. Robert helped to translate our discussion. We spoke about my journey to Uganda, what life was like in my part of the world, and what life was like in their part of the world. I shared pictures of kangaroos and koalas. I spoke of my family, my brothers and sisters. Although it didn't seem like we had much in common, at our core we were all simply humans bonding over our shared values – our love for family, our desire to live a good life, our desire to feel safe and secure and to be loved by others.

During our discussion, Robert explained to me how the support of World Vision empowered the community to become self-sustainable. I heard how the family used their donations to purchase an ox that helped to increase yields of produce on the farm, which Cavin's mother would then sell at the local market. I learned about the family's plan to acquire another small piece of land which would help to facilitate a cooperative initiative and enable community members to gain access to more yields and markets at a reasonable cost. As I listened to their words, I felt so honoured to be in their presence. I felt honoured to learn from them and to have had the opportunity to meet them in a place so far from where I called home.

That afternoon, we participated in traditional song and dance in the open grounds of the compound. At one stage, there would have been over eighty people joining in the celebrations. All the women were dressed in flamboyant colours. The collective energy of the group was emanating joy. The appetising aroma of a spit-roast goat wafted over us as we chanted and moved in a synchronised circular motion, our feet connecting to the earth, her particles of dust dancing around us. The connection I felt at that moment to the people of the village, to Africa and to a greater life purpose was significantly stronger than anything I'd felt in a long time. Those were the moments I was lacking: the presence of community and the feeling of connection.

Humans are a social species. Since the dawn of our existence, we've relied on cooperation to survive and thrive. Yet in more recent years, specifically in Western societies, we've become rather individualistic. Have your own room at six, move out of home at eighteen, have children and keep them inside the confines of their safe and secluded backyards, or walls. They say it takes a village to raise a child, but where had our villages gone? It seemed the modern-day village was now a ten-storey apartment block, and you didn't even know your neighbours on a first-name basis. On some fundamental level, I felt that lack of collectivism, the lack of symbiotic relationships, affected us on levels we weren't able to fully articulate. At least for me, I felt a longing for that sense of community, that interconnectedness.

Back in Sydney, more than two years after my time in Africa, I sat on the floor of Dean's apartment and reflected on the uncomfortable events that happened that day in the office. My body was right, I had to stop. I had to change course.

That evening, I had one of the biggest epiphanies of my life. I wholeheartedly acknowledged that I could no longer spend my life living unaligned with my values. There was no longer a version of me that would settle for that relentless career that lacked the kind of purpose and connection I would soon realise I wanted to dedicate the next years of my life to uncovering.

That acknowledgement, that honouring of my heart's message, led me to open up my personal computer one evening in late autumn and create a document titled *Letter of Resignation*. There, I put both hands on the helm of my ship and subsequently changed the course of my life.

Chapter 6 - A sacrifice

The first law of thermodynamics is that energy can neither be created nor destroyed, only transformed, and so the total amount of energy in existence has always been the same. The universe is all just atoms changing shape, flipping, inverting, reverting, shapeshifting. We are all made of stars and what surrounds us – each and every single particle – is undergoing a magical infinite metamorphosis.

When I made that long-awaited decision to leave my career and flow towards the estuary of an open sea, the energy that had been absorbed by the acute concentration of hours upon hours of mental exertion was now free to alchemise into a future I had not yet experienced. I was an artist with a palette of cosmic colours and an expansive blank canvas to create my masterpiece. *But what to paint?*

It had been so long since I'd felt freedom like that. I could barely remember a time my life wasn't programmed with meetings and never-ending to-do lists, a time when I didn't just live for the weekends. The act of leaving my job triggered an internal culture shock. My entire being was still adjusting to the concept of presence. I'd spend my days sleeping in late to solidify the realisation I didn't have to wake up to that dreaded alarm. I'd cook meals, which was something I rarely did in my life. For the most part, I became a human being, rather than a human doing.

Dean arrived home one evening from a work conference where he was a keynote speaker on digital design and sustainability in construction. He had been working long hours that week, and despite how much he loved his job, I could sense the workload was exhausting him. The smell of two pizzas I had ordered for us welcomed him home. I poured him a large glass of orange juice, sat next to him on the suede grey sofa in the living room, put my hands on his hands, and opened up the space between us for dialogue.

"Do you remember that night in the summer when we wrote down all the things we wanted to achieve in the next ten years?" I asked him.

"I remember," he responded.

"Well, I've been thinking about that list a lot over the past few days. I've decided I want to leave Australia and start to do some of those things, and I would love for you to come with me."

As I held his hands and said those words, I imagined that is what it felt like to ask the person you loved to marry you. Although, I had no ring, and I wasn't down on one knee. Instead, I simply stared into his eyes with eager appeal and asked him to go on a life-changing journey with me.

We sat in silence for a few moments. I sensed both bewilderment and happiness in his facial expression, with a slight tilt towards bewilderment.

"That would be amazing," he responded. "I mean, there are some things we'd have to see about. For example, my work, finances, timings, but I love the idea."

His response filled me with happiness, and I didn't hold back in showing it. I immediately threw myself over his body to embrace him in an entwined hug, knocking over the glass of orange juice in the act. I didn't care though. I was hypnotised by unfathomable euphoria. I had everything I could have ever asked for in the whole entire universe right there, clutched tightly in my arms.

That year, the winter was mild and sunny, with only the morning frost on the windowpane to remind us that the southern hemisphere was tilted away from the sun. Although, on many days, there was seldom a cloud in the sky outside, my mind was full of clouds – cumulus, stratus, cirrus – passing by in a conga-line of sorts, representing thoughts, plans and ideas for the next chapter in our lives together.

In April, to save some money for the trip, Dean and I had moved into the lower section of his mum's family home, a place full of memories from his childhood and teenage years – the framed gridiron jersey he wore when he represented Australia in the under-17s, an inherited antique bar stand made of wood, brass and covered with cowhide, complemented by a more current aluminium Route 66 sign he collected on a Contiki tour through the United States, and a rather peculiar heirloom bar stool made from the foot of a naturally deceased circus elephant. Our premises consisted of a kitchenette, a large living area, access to the back garden and a femininely decorated bedroom, with light-blue wash walls and a white metal bedstead that was more Victorian era than 2015, but it was cosy, nonetheless.

It was kind of Dean's mother to let us stay there with her. Though, I felt she was happy to have the company. The extended four-bedroom home would have been a large domain for just one woman, but she had remained on her own in the property since Dean's father had sadly passed away less than two years prior. I never had the chance to meet Glen. I wished I could have met the man who instilled in Dean the virtuous values that made me love him so dearly.

Throughout our relationship, it was a rare occurrence for Dean to speak in depth about his father. I think the grief he felt sat deeper than the Mariana Trench, beneath the sand, in a corked glass bottle, in a padlocked chest, with a label reading: "Do not open."

On one of those regular evenings when we'd pull profound questions on each other like gunslingers in a duel, I asked him, "What is one word that summarises your life right until this point?" Without as much as a breath, he answered, "Endurance."

In the short timeframe of eighteen months, Dean lost three people incredibly close to him – one of which was his father. Loss was a second shadow he learned to live with. That shadow forced him to grow about ten invisible layers of extraordinary strength that protected all the people around him and held them up when they were falling. He selflessly endured debilitating pain and grief to ease the suffering of the people he loved the most. But I never saw that pain. It was buried in the trench too.

One evening, Dean called me on his way home from work.

"Hey," I answered. "Are you nearby?"

"Yep, and I have a present for you," he said.

"Oooh, it feels like my birthday already," I responded with the glee of a birthday morning.

Dean came through the living room that evening holding a board under one arm and a bag in his other hand. I wondered what was on the board.

He walked towards me. Excitement gleamed in his eyes as he handed me the bag. I opened it to find two balls of string, one red and one fluorescent green, along with a jar of push pins and some coloured sticky notes. My eyes shifted to the board as Dean displayed it to me. It was a map of the world, printed out in colour and pinned to a large corkboard.

"I thought we could use this to plan out all the countries we want to visit," he said.

My smile could have wrapped around that whole world. I was elated. "Thank you!" I said. "This is so thoughtful."

Around the time we started planning our journey, I shared with Dean my idea to expand my blog to focus on community development and the intersection of tourism and sustainability. It was in line with my core values and the Bachelor of International Studies I had enrolled in earlier that year with the hope to open up new pathways of opportunity for myself. One of my modules led me to a book by Australian philosopher, Peter Singer, titled: *The Life You Can Save – Acting Now to End World Poverty*. The book spoke about effective altruism and how we, as individuals, could make intentional choices that increased our impact in this world. It spoke to our collective role in the mission to end poverty and how much was still to be done.

One part of the book specifically resonated with me:

If you are paying for something to drink when safe drinking water comes out of the tap, you have money to spend on things you don't really need. Around the world, a billion people struggle to live each day on less than you paid for that drink.

Singer's words echoed in my soul and the term "altruism" – simply defined as the selfless concern for the well-being of others – went on to become the inspiration behind the title of my next blog, *The Altruistic Traveller*.

The plan was to spend roughly one year abroad starting in Southeast Asia, as it was the closest continent to Australia and, at the time, AirAsia ran a regular flight schedule between Sydney and Kuala Lumpur. I would use my blog as a public medium to share stories and document ways people could incorporate altruism into their travels. I became incredibly attached to the idea. It sparked a fire inside of me fuelled by immense passion.

"I'm thinking we can start in Kuala Lumpur, travel north overland and then cross the border into Thailand," I said, as I placed two pins on the map and connected them with a piece of red string. "And then, we could spend a few months backpacking Southeast Asia, covering Cambodia, Laos and Vietnam. What do you think about the timings in each country? Would three weeks be enough?"

Standing on the cushions of the couch and trying to keep my balance on the squashy surface, I reached up to the board which we had stuck to the wall behind it. I looked over my shoulder at Dean. He was vigilantly watching me paint my canvas. I was emanating the kind of enthusiasm exhibited by an artist given permission to paint anything they wanted with infinite colours.

"You're the more experienced traveller," he said. "I'll let you decide."

He smiled at me and without words acknowledged that my questions were probably rhetorical. He was right, I'd often already preconceived the answers to most of my questions but asked them anyway because I enjoyed talking to him, like any best friend would.

As the weeks went on, the red and green strings filled the map until most of Southeast and Eastern Asia was covered in vibrant, triangular patchwork. I sat and stared at my masterpiece with pride and daydreamed about all the adventures to be had. Dean was working long hours at the office again, so I would spend most of the days at home alone, either studying or planning our itinerary, scouring the internet for social-impact projects to visit in the towns I'd listed sequentially on the shared Google Sheets document I created.

Months went by until one cold, mid-August evening when Dean came home a little later than normal. I figured he'd just missed the usual 17:37 all-stops Illawarra train and so didn't think too much into his delayed arrival. My ears perked to the sound of the front wire door clanging shut around a quarter-past seven in the evening.

"Hi! How was your day? Do you want to order some Thai for dinner?" I greeted him with a kiss on the lips. The closeness of our bodies allowed me to sense a variance in his usual energy.

"Is everything OK?" I asked him, studying his reaction with enhanced focus.

The leather laptop satchel on his shoulder was weighing him down and so he removed it, placed it on the floor and then sat on the couch, but not comfortably; towards the edge as if to signify it wasn't a time to relax.

"There's something I have to tell you," he said. "I … I can't come with you. I can't leave my life here. It's just …well … I have so much here – my job, my family. It doesn't feel right to leave it all behind."

The words flowed anxiously from his lips. I watched them move but anything that followed "I can't come with you" blurred like coloured clothes circulating in a washing machine. Blood drained from my face, dispersing to protect my vital organs as my body's fight or flight response activated. Drunk on cortisol, I attempted a response but all that came out was "Oh …"

"I'm so sorry," he continued.

There was immense remorse in his tone. I wondered how long he had been waiting to tell me this. Although, even if he was showing any signs of doubt, I wouldn't have noticed, consumed by my desire to leave this chapter behind and embark on a journey into the unknown. *Was I so selfishly fixated on my grand idea that I failed to see the obvious hints of hesitation or procrastination indicated by the man I loved?*

I had fantasised the scenes of our future so vividly in my mind, over and over. It was all so promising to me – me the traveller, me the one who imagined her life abroad, me the one who had been dreaming of this change for longer than I had admitted to myself. And then it dawned on me. Dean was following *my* path. He wasn't following the path he had planned. For him, the reckless decision to give up a whole identity, and travel the world indefinitely, seemed fun and adventurous yet, inversely foolish. It suddenly became apparent that, perhaps, the only real force driving his initial agreement to join me was his love for me.

They say all you need is love but I wondered if that was true. When two people aren't walking in the same direction, when two lovers aren't destined for the same port, how long would it take for the distance between them to form a fracture so large it can no longer be bridged?

In the weeks after that evening, as the white, lacy jasmine flowers bloomed across Sydney, subtle cracks formed in the building blocks of our relationship. The deep sadness we were both feeling manifested into frustration, and we began arguing about small, insignificant things to avoid deepening the discussion about what would become of *us*. I didn't want to give up on my plans and I knew if I followed Dean's path, and stayed in Sydney, I would end up in a different kind of unknown destination, an unfamiliar place; a place I may not want to be. We were both hurting. We were both unsure. It was as if we were sitting on opposite ends of a chessboard in a tiebreaker checkmate. There was no easy move. No matter what, one person had to make a sacrifice. No one played, and so the sacrifice was us.

In the common narrative structure of *The Hero's Journey*, one who is called to adventure must cross a threshold from the ordinary, known world into the unknown world. There they will face many tests, including a supreme ordeal they must survive in order for the world in which the hero lives to continue to exist. I wondered, was this ordeal between Dean and I destined to exist in order for the rest of our stories to be written? After all, no great love story ever ended without a sacrifice.

We'd drifted so far apart since the night we stood dancing and dreaming from within our cocoon of comfort. I suppose, by its very nature, a cocoon is a safe and silken cover spun by a creature getting ready to transform. I just always thought we'd transform together. But it seemed that dream was dissolving right before my eyes. Was I ready to do this adventure on my own? I wasn't sure I was capable. All I knew was that the ordeal had caused our hearts to experience the most excruciating affliction of their lives until that point. They shattered into a thousand shards of glass, and we had no choice but to sorrowfully pick them up, hold them gently in our hands and continue our paths separately, along with a straggling hitchhiker named grief.

Chapter 7 - Margaritas

My mother opened the door of the front veranda in her Redlands Bay home and greeted me with a comforting embrace.

"Nice to see you, honey," she said. "Come in. I'll put your things in the bedroom."

I had booked a weekend trip to Australia's north-eastern state of Queensland to bid my family a temporary farewell, as I was not too sure about the timeline of my upcoming adventure, and I had a feeling it would be a while before I would see them again.

A few years earlier, my mother had relocated from Sydney to a suburb about forty minutes southeast of Brisbane. The simpler, laid-back life of the Sunshine State was a more suitable place for her to raise my four teenage half-brothers. Despite the now 900-kilometre distance between us, I quickly got used to having an excuse to head north every now and then to a warmer climate, to feel the fine white sands of the Gold Coast beaches between my toes.

As I unpacked my small khaki rucksack, Mum entered the room.

"How are you feeling after everything that happened?" Her simple words pierced my wounded heart. *How fragile we are in the immaturity of grief.* My eyes welled with tears.

"I don't know." My lips trembled as I spoke. "I don't know if I can do this on my own."

"Oh, honey. You can do this," she answered. "I know it feels like you can't. But I think you need this time on your own to know yourself. You haven't spent any time on your own for a very long time, so it will feel uncomfortable, but I think it will be good for you."

Mum knew everything about my life. I was an open book to her. Her benevolent, unprejudiced nature created a dynamic between us where I felt safe to tell her every single diminutive detail, without hesitation. She would often say to me, "I know my children." She was right. She knew her six children more than we knew ourselves.

"I got you something," she said, as she opened her mirrored sliding wardrobe and reached behind the piles of unfolded clothes, some falling out onto the floor as she pulled out a colourful A4-sized book. She graciously placed it in my hands. I scanned the cover. It read, *Oh, the Places You'll Go!* by Dr Seuss.

"I saw this and had to get it for you. Open it."

On the front page of the book was a handwritten message:

To my baby girl,
Oh, the places you'll go. I'm so proud of you.
Love you forever.
~Your mum
P.S. Stay safe on your travels.

"Thank you, Mum," I said, as I read her genuine words and then flipped through the pages until I landed somewhere in the middle.

Seuss's colourfully bizarre illustrations enmeshed me like a surrealist Dali painting would. His words, even more encapsulating:

You will come to a place where the streets are not marked.
Some windows are lighted. But mostly they're darked.
A place you could sprain both your elbow and chin!
Do you dare to stay out? Do you dare to go in?
How much can you lose? How much can you win?

I had lost. I didn't know what was up ahead. But for the first time in a while, I felt a feeling of enthusiasm. Opening that book and reading those words triggered a déjà vu-like moment. I recalled a conversation I had with someone but couldn't distinguish who it was. They said, "Déjà vu is a sign from the universe that you're on the path you're meant to be walking." I faintly shrugged off the feeling but didn't throw it away, like a receipt left in the bottom of a winter coat. Despite the sadness that sat beside me, I felt hopeful about the future.

Back in Sydney, I began to organise my life for a year abroad. It had been over a month since I painfully moved my belongings from the home Dean and I shared and into my father's house, back to the bedroom I spent much of my teenage years in. Those pale peach walls spoke of intangible memories, the contents of my wardrobe bore tangible ones. I commenced rummaging through drawers to discard meaningless artefacts that had been collecting dust over the course of many years. Some of the remnants included old costume jewellery, threadbare shoes, an old-fashioned purse I took to my year 10 formal, an expendable Canon camera from the years when AAA batteries were in demand. For a woman not yet 30, I had accumulated enough junk to run a garage sale for the suburb, and this was despite a challenge I had undertaken a few years prior to refrain from buying any new clothes for one year. I called it my Year of Second-hand, and the mission was to raise awareness about the horrendous social and environmental impact caused by our society's mindless over-consumption and obsession to acquire material wealth. I had wished my awareness of the topic sprouted fifteen years earlier when I was naively consumed by the desire to look as pretty as the girls on the cover of *Dolly* and *Cosmopolitan* magazines. Their bright, matte portraits hypnotised me into a brainwashed state of "I'll have what she's having" and turned me into bait for a capitalist society to feed on. At least I eventually grew up to advocate against such nonsense.

There's a cognitive shift that occurs when you endeavour to spend a whole year living out of a backpack – a realisation that one doesn't need an accumulation of a lifetime's belongings to get from one day to the next. The decluttering of my worldly possessions at that time was a salient contrast to a shift occurring in my story. There was a costume change in my stage play. An '*Action!*' to the next scene of my life.

As I laid out pieces of clothing in a 'take' pile on the duvet which covered my bed, I heard the vibration of my mobile phone. The phone lit up with a cartoon character image of a girl with glistening eyes the colour of a shallow ocean, shoulder-length black hair and a smiling cat. It was my friend, Amy. Some time ago, we'd generated cartoon avatars of ourselves and made them our profile images on the phone. Amy loved her cats more than anything in the world.

"Hey!" she said. "How are you?"

"I'm OK. Just trying to fit my whole life into a 50-litre backpack," I quipped.

"Come with me to Reggae Sundays at Hive Bar this weekend. I want to spend as much time as I can with you before you go on your big adventure," she said.

I was so appreciative of my friends' support regarding the journey I was about to embark on. At the time, I was a frightened, heartbroken girl who had just erased her canvas to start a new life that went against everything she'd ever known until that point. My friends believed in me more than I believed in myself, and their love became a powerful weapon against my own self-doubt.

The Hive Bar was a buzzy hole-in-the-wall venue situated on a corner of Sydney's inner-west suburb of Erskineville. On Sundays, the venue would support local artists by allowing them to take over the decks and pierce rhythms into the souls of patrons who occupied the sparse mezzanine as a salute to the weekend.

"Another margarita?" I said to Amy as I licked the remnants of salt from my lips.

"Sure," she replied.

I walked up to the bar to order some drinks for Amy and me, leaning my arms on the mahogany counter. The bartender approached me. His smile was as warm as the sun's rays hitting your cheeks on a winter's day. He had dark sandy, blonde hair that curled and reached the top of his right eyebrow and was wearing a light-blue buttoned shirt, with phoenix-shaped maroon birds printed throughout. His demeanour was poised, yet modest.

"What can I get you?" he asked.

"I'll take two margaritas, please," I responded with an unintentional coquettish smile.

We engaged in some small-talk while I watched him perform his mixology. There was an inherent cheerfulness to his energy, and I found myself fixated on him for longer than a few seconds.

"There you go," he said as he gently placed the two margaritas on the bar-top. "That'll be twelve dollars."

I took the margaritas back to the table, sat down opposite Amy and attempted to share about my oddly engrossing encounter.

"I just had a weird moment with the bartender," I explained to her as I pushed the slice of lime from the brim of my cup and into its contents. "I think we were flirting."

It felt unnatural to even say those words. It had been less than a few months since Dean and I separated and we were still in contact, trying to figure out if there were any pieces of our love we could salvage and glue back together. Still, I was confused about what the future held for us and, on top of that, I was consumed by feelings of abandonment and disappointment. But as the tequila and Cointreau entered my bloodstream that afternoon, loose-fitting plasters masked my gaping wounds and I sat present with my friend, listening to the uplifting beats of reggae music and reminiscing on times gone by.

Amy returned from another round trip to the bar. She placed the last margarita for the evening on the table beside me and looked at me with a suggestive smirk.

"I have something for you," she said.

As the words left her mouth, she placed a folded cocktail napkin in front of me. I examined it for a moment, picked it up and unfolded it gently. There in neat black handwriting was the bartender's name and phone number, *Conor.*

The next day, I sat on my bed and stared at the napkin in front of me the way a child would stare at a cookie jar on the top cupboard shelf, presumptuously, knowing they weren't allowed to access it but curious as to what apparatus they could build in order to climb those cupboards and reach for the jar. Receiving that paper napkin provoked in me the first romantic feeling I'd experienced since my heart had ruptured. The subsequent dopamine hit jerked me into a heedless version of myself I hardly knew. And without further ado, I opened the messaging application on my mobile phone and reached into the cookie jar.

It's a natural reaction for humans to avert emotional pain and trauma. Why sit with pain when we can choose to circumvent it? That's probably why industries built on the demands of humans numbing their pain make for lucrative business models, and why Prohibition ultimately failed. And why, these days, you can be prescribed antidepressants faster than you can order a cheeseburger from McDonald's drive-thru. It's apparent our species tends to take the path of least resistance.

A part of me questioned whether becoming involved with Conor so soon after my relationship with Dean was a hasty decision that would backfire. But he swiftly became my respite. The more we spent time together, the more his earthy nature secured me like a rain tree sheltering me from a storm.

Conor grew up in sub-tropical Far North Queensland. He was a country boy who moved to the city and never lost his green thumb. I think it was that bohemian, free-spiritedness that attracted me to him. He would inquisitively ask me about my writing, my philanthropic work, about the times I backpacked through India, Cambodia, Europe and East Africa. He was three years younger than me, and I sensed, in a way, that he looked up to me. It made me feel admired.

"You know, I am leaving in less than a month," I said to him, staring deeply into his hazel eyes.

When we met, I was honest about my situation: about my plan to spend a year abroad. But he still insisted on meeting each other on multiple occasions until that point, and I never declined the offers.

As we spoke at dinner that evening, I felt my phone vibrating in my jeans pocket. I ignored it at first, but it rang again. My heart skipped a beat. I knew the person on the other end of the line was Dean, and I had omitted to tell him that I was seeing Conor. I was petrified of hurting him. I should have told him sooner, but I didn't know how to explain everything. I was confused. I was going through an intense period of change, experiencing feelings I'd never experienced before. I was upset at Dean but also still in love with him, and now befuddled by new feelings emerging for someone else. My life had never felt so much like an overly dramatic soap opera.

I let the calls ring out that evening and didn't call back until the following day.

"Hi," I said softly, heart pounding so rapidly I could see my chest rising.

"Were you with someone last night?" he asked, abruptly.

I knew he knew. I sensed anger in his voice, but it wasn't anger. It was impairing sadness.

"Yes," I replied, my words piercing his heart with the strength of a hundred nails. He hung up there and then. When I tried to call back to explain myself, my number was blocked.

Chapter 8 - Goodbyes

The two backpacks I had filled with clothes, toiletries, electronics, hopes, dreams and aspirations sat neatly by my bedroom door. My Australian passport lay on top, the only thing separating me from the shores I grew up on and the great wide world.

"I guess this is everything," I said to my dad as he watched his eldest daughter prepare for one of the biggest experiences of her life.

He probably hoped I was preparing for a different kind of experience. A wedding, perhaps. The birth of his first grandchild. But instead, he observed me in silence, hiding the fact my sudden departure left him apprehensive. I think it was still quite a shock to him that at almost thirty, I'd quit my job and bought a one-way ticket to Malaysia. I was sure part of him wished he could convince me to stay, but my wings weren't to be clipped. I was his unfettered hatchling, his hard-headed firstborn. All he could do in those moments was let me fly.

No one prepares you for the selflessness necessary to not only raise your children but also support and encourage them to be the truest versions of themselves, even if it means watching them walk out the door, not knowing when you will see them again.

"You just come back whenever you want to, OK?" he said, with a cogent tone. "And if you need anything, you just call us, you hear? Anything at all."

The "us" he was referring to were my Maltese family – Dad's brother and sister who lived in the semi-detached home next door. Needless to say, bringing a traditional Mediterranean dynamic to our lives. My uncle and auntie played a predominant role in my upbringing. Neither of them had their own children but they treated my sister and me, and our two cousins, Frank and Andrew, as if we were their own; supporting us in all facets of our lives. Although my parents separated when I was three years old, instead of feeling as though I'd lost a parent, I was fortunate to gain two.

I had fond memories of sleepovers the four of us cousins would have as children in the three-bedroom apartment where my dad, auntie, uncle, nanna and nanno lived when they emigrated from Malta to Australia in the early eighties. I spent almost every second weekend there throughout my early childhood until my teenage years.

We would play hide-and-seek around the bounds of the property. We'd argue who got the front seat in the Valiant on the drive to watch my dad referee soccer at the Mascot Kings Football Club, mostly so we could get hotdogs at the end of the games. I learned to ride a bicycle in the driveway beneath those red-brick walls. We would entertain ourselves by playing with marbles on the concrete grounds under the hills hoist in the back yard, as my uncle gutted *rizzi* (sea urchin) under the running water of the garden tap and my auntie hung the towels to dry. Occasionally, we would take turns playing Alex The Kid on the Sega Master System to see who could progress Alex further towards his goal of saving his brother Egle from the evil king Janken, by winning some suspenseful games of scissors, paper, rock. And on the days the scorching Australian sun heated the interior of the non-airconditioned apartment, we'd fill up water balloons and fluorescent super soakers and play cops and robbers until dusk brought about a cool breeze, or the occasional summer afternoon thunderstorm laid the heat to rest.

It had been interesting growing up as a second-generation child. I was able to observe the contrasting subtleties between Australian culture and Maltese culture and see how they manifested in the nature of the people and situations around me. Australians were generally untroubled in nature, jaunting through life with an airy attitude. The words "no worries" occupied a frequent share of the Australian vocabulary, complemented by an indifferent attitude towards most things except cricket scores and housing prices. For the Maltese, worry was an alter ego. There's a Maltese proverb that says "*Ahseb fil-hazin halli t-tajjeb ma jonqos.*" In English, it translates to "think of the bad so that the good will not fail." Perhaps the lesser tendency for the Maltese to fixate on optimism was a result of generational trauma induced by an extensive history of warfare. From the Norman Invasion to the Great Siege of Malta, to the more recent World War I and II, the rock they call "the jewel of the Mediterranean" and her honourable, resilient people had withstood a substantial amount of conflict. Yet an inspirational comradery united the Maltese. They would go to great lengths to protect the people they loved, especially when it came to family. And I admired that sense of family, no matter how vexatious it felt at times.

It was ironic how my Maltese family's immoderate concern for my well-being ultimately perpetuated my courage to leave Australia in the first place. Their love planted a subconscious awareness in me that no matter how far I fell or what went wrong, there would always be someone to catch me before I hit the ground. At the time, I didn't see how much their protection guided me because I felt bitterly misunderstood. I had dubbed myself the black sheep of the family and become quite reclusive because I felt that my unconventional behaviour didn't live up to their expectations of me. I wasn't married, I wasn't thinking about having children. I didn't have a secure job or any job at all. I didn't even have a long-term partner anymore. Those were the benchmarks I felt measured against to be accepted by them.

With hindsight, it was no fault of theirs or mine. It was remnants of a thousand years of patriarchy. Bygone generations being told their worthiness came from their status in society, the colour of their skin, the surname on their birth certificate, the pennies in their pockets. We were all still in the process of ridding ourselves of those redundant ideologies like cleaning coffee stains off fine china.

Despite the feelings of inadequacy I felt around my family at that time, I never attempted to explain myself to them. Instead, I concealed the truest parts of me: my love for writing; my dreams of changing the world, exploring far corners of this earth and adding new perspectives to my collections, next to the stamps and fridge magnets. I sat silently at gatherings, commenting on the weather or any other shallow topic that allowed me to deflect personal questions warranting personal answers. I never fully explained why I felt called to leave Australia, why I left my job, or the real reason why Dean and I parted ways. I simply remained silent, enclosing my truth in trapdoors. I convinced myself that although they loved me, it was conditional.

My wilful suppression ultimately obscured the parts of myself I desperately wanted them to know, see and acknowledge. Although, at the time, I didn't have the wisdom or discernment required to understand that the less I spoke my truth, the less I was giving them a chance to see who I really was and, in turn, accept me for who I was. Instead of permitting that opportunity, I kept myself small. The subsequent consequence that occurs when we keep ourselves small is that the space we occupy diminishes and, eventually, we aren't able to be seen at all. It's not until we unapologetically step into our wholeness, our plumage on full display – the way a performer steps confidently, defiantly, onto a stage – that we offer others the ability to meet us as we are.

It would be many years before that young, diffident girl would learn this lesson, and so I carried nugatory judgement in that backpack with me. It weighed more than the shirts and pants.

In the days before my departure, my inbox overflowed with messages of support. I was so thankful to receive such thoughtful gifts, cards and well wishes for my journey ahead. One of the cards read, "She believed she could, so she did," providing the reminder I needed as nerves began swelling in my stomach. Some were nerves of excitement, some were nerves guided by fear: the fundamental human emotion that, when not controlled, inhibits us from stepping into our purpose, into our alignment. I thought about the succeeding words of Jim Carrey's speech, "You can spend your whole life imagining ghosts, worrying about the pathway to the future, but all there will ever be is what's happening here, and the decisions we make at this moment, which are based in either love or fear."

Despite those feelings of fear that morning and in the preceding months, I solemnly chose to step forward with love.

On 10 November, I walked eagerly through the customs department of Sydney Kingsford Smith International Airport, each step a word in my new narrative. But no matter how much I looked at the pages ahead, I couldn't avoid the painful feeling as though a page was missing, torn from the spine of my story. Dean occupied the seats in my mind. *He should have been here.* My heart still ached.

I watched as the gate for my flight was allocated. Kuala Lumpur, 22:35, Gate 22. I wanted to call him, to hear his voice, to share that moment with him just like I had imagined all those months before. I thought about calling and then thought not to call. And then thought about calling again, going back and forth, a dance of indecision. Eventually, I gave in and dialled his number.

I put the phone to my ear only to be met with the humdrum sounds of a broken line.

"Flight AK713 ready for boarding." I heard the flight announcement over the speaker.

As I walked through the jet bridge, I breathed out. I knew it was time to let go. A tear rolled down my cheek. I released any feelings of sadness and switched my perspective to gratitude. For the first time, I selflessly acknowledged my bravery and recognised how far I'd come – how every single unyielding decision in the preceding year had led me to that point. I knew once that plane left the tarmac my life would never be the same. It was already changing. Yesterday was already gone. The foregoing breath was already gone. I pondered about how each moment is a chance for us to write the next word in our story, to change our narrative. *Life is a trillion fleeting moments like this one.* I was ready for whatever was to come next.

Before take-off, I sat comfortably on the plane with my seatbelt fastened. Prompted by the airline's request to switch off electronic devices, I picked up my mobile phone to trigger aeroplane mode. There I saw an email notification. It was from Dean. My heart skipped a beat.

Dear Bianca,

You're probably on the plane right now. I couldn't bring myself to call you. I know you've moved on and I think it's best we stop contacting each other so we can both move forward in our new lives.

I think of us like Shakespeare's Romeo and Juliet, a star-crossed love destined to never be because the world wouldn't allow it. But instead of us dying in the end it was our relationship. Even though we joked about the space-time continuum collapsing because we had met, I think it could have, like an unsolvable equation that questions everything that man knew. I guess the world just wasn't ready for us this time. Maybe, in the future, we could be a planned pair, but until then we will walk our own paths knowing we had that moment in time where our love defied all universal logic.

Keep doing what you're doing – write, experience and have connections to the people you meet. That truly is a fulfilled life.

~Dean

As I read his unfeigned words, they sounded out in my mind as though it was his voice speaking to me. Tears flowed down my cheeks, dripping onto my heart's centre, mending a piece of it. And as I watched the ground beneath me drift further and further away, metamorphosing into a motherboard of houses and highways, I found comfort in knowing that although the journey was mine now, a part of him was still with me.

Chapter 9 - Borders

I disembarked in Kuala Lumpur (KL) beneath a smoggy, silver sky. The moist, humid air hit my face the way it would after opening an oven door to a meal ready to devour. *Hello again Asia, you fascinating, cultural, tropical continent. Nice to see you.*

There was something about the distant rings of tooting motorbikes and the faint scent of burnt gasoline that acquainted me with that part of the world. I had always been fascinated by Southeast Asia after visiting the region on a few separate occasions in previous years. It was the closest continent to Australia I felt offered tantalising and contrasting characteristics, which exceedingly varied from country to country. I felt it a safer destination, in comparison to some of its counterparts, having not been, in recent years, troubled by war or famine. This enabled many of the countries in the region to experience significant economic development, which in turn stimulated tourism economies and improved the living conditions of its residents. I felt Southeast Asia was the right place to start my journey to discover stories and initiatives worth sharing with the world. Plus, it made up the majority of the fluorescent-string treasure map I created all those months before. If I was still endeavouring to follow that map.

Standing beneath the arrival gate C of KLIA2 in Malaysia's capital, I opened the CouchSurfing app on my phone and searched for the inbox icon to message my soon-to-be host, Ira. CouchSurfing was a social networking service and one of the first mobile applications that leveraged advanced technologies to improve the way people travelled. The platform facilitated connections between travellers and hosts willing to offer their couches, or in some cases rooms, to those who needed a place to stay. The multi-sided marketplace enabled hosts and travellers to list their profiles and match with one another according to interests, travel dates and property types. Users could leave reviews, access identity validation and message one another through the app to adhere to safety regulations. At the time, there was no payment required other than the return of a hospitable favour if the opportunity ever arose, so it was quite an innovative idea and a rather remarkable exchange of generosity by those in the community. It was also widely appealing to a budget traveller like me.

CouchSurfing was one of the many strategies I planned to implement to keep my travels at a minimal cost. I wasn't earning an income anymore, and so the money I had needed to last me as long as possible. In the beginning, it was mildly uncomfortable to watch the figures in my bank account ever so gradually decline, like sand through an hourglass, instead of seeing incremental figures on the second Wednesday of every month. But I slowly became used to it. We're adaptable creatures, us humans.

On some level, I was curious as to what it would feel like to not rely on a paycheck every week, to not be a pawn on the chessboard of this economic game. I wanted to, for a short while, throw that security blanket off me and walk without its heavy weight. Indeed, it was a privilege to forego a paycheck to learn about the correlation between money and happiness; nevertheless, this choice was a reward for me. I was taking a hiatus, a sabbatical. It was time for the caged bird to fly. And so, I ensured myself I would do whatever I could to make the hard-earned reserves I had prudently stashed away last as long as possible. Even if that meant sleeping on a stranger's couch in the bustling city of KL.

Ira was a Muslim Malaysian girl born to a Chinese mother and a Malaysian father, an example of the variety of nationalities that resided in that city. KL was a melting pot of cultural diversity, housing people from all different backgrounds: Indian, Bangladeshi, Chinese, Malaysian, Indonesian, Iranian, you name it. Their presence was complemented by an immense array of cuisines and cultures, beliefs and practices all there within that 243-kilometre radius. It took a few returns to that city to fully appreciate its heterogeneity. I had to first become accustomed to the intense big-city energy and then learn to not look at KL on a macroscopic scale, but rather notice its inherent microcosms are what truly makes it special: rural enclaves like Kampung Baru, hawkers havens like Chow Kit, spirited underground art scenes, unswerving activist movements, a welcoming street food vendor at any hour of the day ready to serve you a plate of nasi lemak or assam laksa that feeds the soul.

Ira picked me up from the Serdang Raya MRT train station and greeted me the way one would greet an old friend. She was a pretty woman in her mid-twenties, with perfectly unblemished, light-toned skin, big warm brown eyes and full lips, wearing a beige-coloured *tudung* (headscarf) atop smart-casual attire.

"Welcome to Malaysia," she said as we manoeuvred our way through the throng of commuters.

It was peak hour in KL and it swiftly became clear to me why their train system was appropriately named MRT – Mass Rapid Transit.

"Let me take something for you," Ira offered.

She kindly took my rucksack and guided me through to the exit of the station.

"My home is a 15-minute walk from here," she said.

We arrived at Ira's apartment and was grateful to learn I had my own single-occupant private quarter in her home for the next few days, as opposed to a couch in the living room. That was always a luxury in the CouchSurfing community. It made you feel the same way you would on the improbable occasion you ever got upgraded to business class on a flight. You knew it was unlikely but did an internal dance when it happened.

"I need to go in to work now but I'll be finished at around five this afternoon and would love to invite you out for dinner with some friends," she said. "Here is a spare set of keys. Message me if you need anything."

"That sounds great," I replied, slightly fatigued from my red-eye flight. "I would love to join you. Send me the address and I'll let you know if I have any trouble getting there. Thank you so much for your hospitality."

Ira closed the door behind her. I sat on the bed for a moment and paused to take it all in. It had been less than twenty-four hours and my world had already changed immensely. *Go to sleep in Sydney. Wake up in Kuala Lumpur.*

I was so happy to be there in that foreign space. I was so grateful for this woman who had aided my journey, the way one would offer water to a thirsty, lone traveller back in the days before motorised transport, perhaps even before the pioneering wheel was invented and people took arduous journeys on foot. There was a commendable level of trust already formed between Ira and me. I deeply admired that, although it went against much of the messaging drummed into me as a child and into my adult life. I had the words *don't talk to strangers* stuck to my temporal lobe like chewing gum to a writing desk. A few days earlier, I received the strong, albeit solicitous, words of advice, "Don't trust anybody!" It was difficult to step forward with this advice and also with an open heart. I felt they contradicted each other; the way love and fear do. Although I understood the origins of concern, I wondered how much of that intentional shielding ultimately perpetuated a division from others, hamstringing any chance of deep connection and oneness.

That evening, I completed an MRT gauntlet to arrive at KL's notorious Bukit Bintang district and met with Ira and her two friends, Iman and Ehsan, brothers of Iranian descent. We chose a popular *mamak* (restaurant) serving Malay Indian cuisine, bringing Indian spices and cooking techniques into traditional Malaysian dishes. Our concoction of heritage at the dinner table that night mimicked the blends of herbs and spices in our meals – an Australian girl born to an Australian mother of Scottish descent and a Maltese father. A Malaysian girl born to a Chinese mother and a Malaysian father, and two Iranian boys born to a Persian mother and a Malaysian father. Despite the differences in where we came from, how we were raised and what we believed in, we engaged in engrossing discussions without judgement, covering an array of topics from political and environmental issues to personal anecdotes and chucklesome stories. It was our differences that united us.

Difference had been an underlying theme in the human story for the most part of my lived experience and, as far as I was aware, the last few millennia. It fuelled war, violence and persecution. That year in 2015, Saudi Arabia had launched airstrikes in neighbouring Yemen to protest against the minority Shiite sect, Houthi, who received support from Iran, Saudi Arabia's mortal enemy. Across borders, Russia was conducting airstrikes on Syria, Boko Haram militants razed towns in north-east Nigeria, ISIS terrorists struck on three continents, and millions of refugees continued to flee across Europe in search of safety. Back on my home soil of Australia, men in suits and ties enforced inhumane asylum seeker policies that saw innocent people locked in offshore detention centres. Their crime – seeking international protection. This issue had always struck a chord with me. Not only as an advocate for human rights but merely as a compassionate person who believed people were inherently good, a girl who sincerely dreamed of a world undivided.

As I sat there at the table with my new friends, I felt further perplexed by how, in so many parts of the world, our differences manifested into hate or fear. I was old enough to have witnessed the subtle ways in which we absorbed this fear from our external environments; how governing bodies and media outlets used this hate and fear to control the masses, strengthen their ratings and line their pockets. Fear was the kryptonite of the human soul. It leaked on us like crude oil in pristine waters.

I discussed a precise example of this in an essay I wrote in relation to Australia's asylum seeker policies. It read,

... The misconception that people from countries afflicted with violence are associated with terrorism, rather than being victims of terrorism, is a stereotype that has forged a public opinion of people that have fled to Australia as asylum seekers. The media is a major influence on this misconception. The 2001 'Children Overboard' scandal was an example of how the media can manipulate not only the perceptions of the public but also the outcome of people's opinions in relation to asylum seekers.

In 2001, after a Norwegian vessel named the Tampa intercepted a boat carrying 433 asylum seekers, the discussion of the asylum seeker policy in Australia rapidly escalated and began to generate widespread media coverage and social debate. John Howard, who was acting Prime Minister at the time, refused to let the Tampa enter Australian waters and took a stand against a "threat to border security" by sending in the Australian navy. Through media coverage and publicity of this event, the conception of asylum seekers transformed from an immigration issue to an issue relating to national security. It was through this conception that the political agenda became apparent. Over the week of the Tampa, John Howard's approval ratings had rocketed 10 points.

When surveyed about some of the fears associated with immigration, the main responses from Australians were "fear of losing job opportunities over pay disputes," "fear of higher unemployment" and "fear of overcrowding" ...

I saw this story as an exemplar that rippled across this world. There was a mass othering of sorts, widening ridges between a population inherently equal. Turn us inside-out and we all contain the same contents: one heart, a city of veins, bare bones. Yet, fear plagued us, often unwittingly, and the consequences of that fear affected innocent people – people like Kurdish-Iranian journalist Behrouz Boochani, who spent almost seven years detained in a detention centre on Manus Island after coming to Australia by boat. During his imprisonment, he wrote the award-winning book, *No Friend But The Mountains*, a heart-wrenching recount of a perilous journey across borders. While reading that book, I thought about my own father's ability to emigrate across borders at a time when Australia welcomed immigrants to their 'boundless plains to share'. That journey ultimately brought me into this world. I was a borderless child, fortunate to be born into a country with a passport strong enough to allow me to then step foot outside of those borders and safely return, if and when I pleased. I would often wonder what afforded me those rights and not others. It piled on top of the huge stack of unjust intricacies about this world I couldn't comprehend.

Nevertheless, I was grateful to hear the vast array of perspectives about those intricacies, the just and unjust sides of this complex polygon. Every encounter, like the one in the mamak in KL, expanded my worldview and left a mark on me, engraved next to the freckles on my arms.

I spent the next few days exploring the streets of KL, acclimatising to the muggy air, my taste buds on a culinary journey of their own. It was the days when Google Maps' accuracy was substandard and so my quest for specific restaurants almost always left me meandering down concrete footpaths and into local hole-in-the-wall eateries. I felt like an ant navigating its way through the corridors of an ant's nest. That city was so much larger than me.

I then journeyed beyond the boisterous confines of Malaysia's capital and headed north to the greener pastures of the Cameron Highlands, a plateau region known for its tea estates, farmlands and mossy forests. Several buses ran daily from Bandar Tasik Selatan train station and so I took the overland four-hour journey through winding roads and over mountains to be met with some of the most magnificent landscapes I'd witnessed in my life until that point. There were vast fields of iridescent green plantations as far as my eyes could see, verdant mountainous ranges as their backdrop. The colours of the foliage altered depending on the reflection of the sky – emerald, lime, shamrock, olive. Perfectly formed hedges blanketed the fields like tiny mazes. I could no longer feel the heavy water vapour in the atmosphere. Instead, my trachea welcomed cool, crisp breaths of fresh air. I felt it all the way to my lungs.

I spent my days trekking through the mossy forests, sampling tea at locally owned cafés or famous tea plantations like Boh Plantation. I would spend my evenings at the Orchid Haven Guesthouse, speaking with other travellers from various continents across the globe. Sometimes, a group of us would share a Malaysian steamboat meal together in the local town of Tanah Rata where we would sit at a traditional round table around a Chinese-style fondue and collectively place raw meat, fish and vegetables to cook in the boiling broth. Life had begun to seem rather effortless.

That November, I descended the highlands, travelled towards the Malaysian coastline, past the street murals of Penang's historical capital, George Town, across the Strait of Malacca to the pristine *pantai* (beaches) of Langkawi and then back into the beating heart of KL. By the end of the month, I'd crossed the border and landed in Thailand's capital, Bangkok. Or as the Thais call it, *Krung Thep Maha Nakhon* (great city of angels).

Thailand felt, to me, like the matriarch of Southeast Asia. Tourism boomed there when Leonardo DiCaprio swooned us with his blue eyes and sun-kissed hair on a defiant expedition to the immaculate Maya Bay in the 2000 film, *The Beach*. The film's ensuing publicity influenced the number of tourists flocking to Thailand and tourism soon became a large contribution to the country's gross domestic product, catapulting them into economic growth.

There was an alluring subliminal message beneath the plot of that movie. It spoke to the parts in us yearning for a paradise, a desire for flawlessness. Moreover, it showed us how that same desire, when not controlled, could lead us to adversity. Just as Richard eventually uncovered the flaws in his exquisite mirage, the subsequent real-life desire to grasp such a paradise ultimately led to the demise of that paradise and by 2018, more than eighty percent of the coral around Maya Bay had been destroyed – a consequence of over-tourism. I hadn't put Maya Bay on my itinerary for that exact reason. Over-tourism was a concept I was advocating against in the least hypocritical way I could have, having been a tourist in my own right. The notion of sustainable tourism was the foundation of my writing at the time, and that talked to the spectrum of social and environmental implications tourism had on global destinations.

Sustainable tourism, by definition, is tourism that minimises negative social, economic and environmental impacts and generates greater economic benefits for local people. It is a spotlight on a trillion-dollar industry that often perpetuates inequalities, exploitation, and environmental degradation. Increased populations in destinations result in higher amounts of pollution, specifically in areas with untreated sewage and unmanaged waste disposal. In the more recent years of the tourism boom, destinations such as Maya Bay in Thailand, Boracay in the Philippines and Kuta in Indonesia have suffered immense environmental damage to their pristine beaches. So much so that governments have begun to implement off-season closures with the aim to allow the regeneration of the ecosystems.

As a subsequent organic evolution to the theme of my blog at the time, the focus on sustainable tourism seemed fitting as it aligned with the concept of social impact. As I read more about those developments, I changed the way I travelled. Wherever I placed my feet, the voice in my head would follow. She would ask, "What kind of impact am I making here? How can I tread with openness, compassion and integrity?" It was through that awareness and curiosity that my journey grew an extra level of consciousness, and I used that consciousness throughout my blog and in my journalism at the time.

I'd arrived in Thailand just in time for the yearly Loy Krathong festival, a significant event occurring throughout Thailand and in nearby countries on the full-moon day of the 12th lunar month. It was a day for believers to pay respects to Buddha and seek forgiveness from the goddess of water for any misdeeds against her. In more modern times, it was a day to honour ancestors and offer prayers to them in return for blessings and guidance.

I opened up my mobile phone to a Meetup event invitation triggered by one of the Southeast Asia backpacker Facebook groups I joined to keep in-the-know while travelling the region. The invitation read:

If you have no plan and want to experience traditional Loy Krathong festival with a local and in the local area, please feel free to join us.

Best wishes,

Kob Khun Khaaaaaaaaaaa!

~Jekky

I was intrigued.

That afternoon, on my first day in the city, as a transient downpour cleared the steamy air, I made my way to Jekky's homestay in Bangkok's central district of Phaya Thai. Upon arrival, I was welcomed by a rather noticeable sign placed across the front of the entrance to the building that read in big handwritten capital letters: 'You've come all this way, welcome home.'

I was joined by roughly nine other participants. Some were friends of Jekky. Others, like me, had newly arrived in the city as curious travellers seeking to immerse themselves in a unique part of Thai culture. On an adjacent table on the front patio of Jekky's residence, she had set up all one would need to construct their own krathong (a small floating container fashioned of leaves and used as an offering). There were cylinder banana tree slices that would be used to form the base of the krathong, strips of two-inch-wide banana leaves to be used to make the petals, and yellow and orange marigold flowers to provide the finishing decorations.

We commenced assembling our offerings for the ceremony ahead. Like children in an art class, we folded coarse strips of banana leaves into what resembled the petals of a lotus flower and carefully pushed toothpicks through the makeshift lotus, and into the banana trunk to keep the leaves in place. I thought back to the last time I'd crafted like that. It would have been years. Surely not over a decade, I dolefully pondered. The creative child in me had waited stagnantly, suppressed by the incessant responsibilities of adulthood. *Achieve one goal and on to the next one.* Adulthood seemed to draw us out of the present moment like dogs chasing their tails. Creativity came last on the list behind the more productive activities like grocery shopping, house cleaning and checking emails. Or the not-so-productive activities like scrolling through social media feeds. Somewhere along the way, we'd lost the ability to slow down, to simply spend an afternoon watching the clouds go by and noticing which animals they looked like – or assembling a krathong for a spiritual offering.

After we'd marvelled at our krathong masterpieces, Jekky invited us to sit and enjoy a home-cooked Thai meal. We gathered around low-lying bamboo tables and sat down on traditional Thai floor cushions made of multicoloured sleeves with kapok filling. Eating while sitting on the floor was a traditional practice still found in parts of southeast and eastern Asian cultures. It was one of the intricate practices that deeply connected me with the Thai culture. I recalled how I would frequent a Thai restaurant in Melbourne's Brunswick every time I visited the city just to dine on the cushioned floor seating. The restaurant's acclaimed pad thai was an added temptation.

Jekky walked into the room with a large pot of red curry in her hands. The smell of lemongrass and coconut milk spoke to my taste buds as I watched her place the pot on the placemat in the middle of our table. The curry was accompanied by a rather distinct serving of blue rice.

"This is butterfly pea rice," she said. "The blue colour comes from the petals of *bunga telang* – the butterfly pea flowers which are used as a natural food colouring. Bon appétit!"

We served ourselves portions of the curry and, once again, strangers became friends over a shared meal, prepared with love and kindness.

That evening, our group ventured to the banks of Bangkok's Chao Phraya River – Thailand's principal river that flowed from the Nakhon Sawan province in northern Thailand and emptied into the Gulf of Thailand, breathing life onto all in its path. The riverbank was swarming with crowds of people. White-topped gazebos lined nearby pathways selling offerings of flowers, rice, incense and candles. The woody smell of the incense transported me back to the days I sat in church as a young child admiring the lovely murals painted on the enormous walls of the school's chapel, on the rare occurrence the murals weren't picturing brutal, gory scenes of bloodshed. At least the Buddhist depictions of spiritual history, displayed in Bangkok's abundance of intricately designed wats (temples), were cartooned in such a way as to warrant a G rating: General audiences.

There was a sacredness to the burning of incense. No matter the culture, tradition or belief system, the fragrant aromas travelled through our nostrils and triggered a response in the brain that could evoke a state of meditation, reflection or peace. Having been considered one of the first fragrant materials to be used by humans, perhaps, on some biological level, our brains made a correlation between this perceptible smell and the concept of spirituality.

At least, for me, there on the banks of the Chao Phraya as I placed my offering down on the silky water reflecting the illumination of fairy lights wrapped around nearby trees, I tapped into something spiritual. I placed my imperfectly handmade krathong onto the river and, like the thousands of riverside pilgrims among me, I prayed. I prayed for the safety of my friends and family, I prayed for the safety of the world. I prayed for Mother Earth, and I prayed for myself.

Dear ancestors, dear river, dear Buddha, or to whom it may concern,

Please guide me on this journey into the unknown. Lend me the courage and strength to keep moving forward. Please show me the way.

Thank you.

I wasn't sure if I should finish with an "amen." Although I was raised Catholic, I no longer considered myself religious. I would say I was more agnostic, or rather an omnist – in the sense that I believed in something bigger than myself and felt aligned to certain messaging behind religious teachings but was generally open and flexible in my faith. I had repudiated Christianity many years beforehand when the walls of my mind could no longer be painted in black and white. I wanted to explore the limitless hues of knowledge and wisdom and spirituality not only prevalent in a mere 2000-year history. Some of my favourite conversations were fed by the incessant curiosity I had about human belief systems. My friend, Rob, shared these words with me during one of our frequent ethereal maunderings. I felt it summed up quite well my desire to look outside the lines of that cognitive square and see it was not a square, but multidimensional in form:

The written word often exposes more insight into humanity when you look at how, when and why it changes when revised, or overwritten, by people in the past; in order to contextualise its meaning and significance. The term for this is palimpsest. When aspects of human history are viewed in this way, we gain the potential to expose deep and chronological meaning within the branches of religions, lore and myth that stretch across the planet, and within the timeless soul of human existence and experience. Once words are set and organised into a 'doctrine' of theology, contextual relationships become crystalline in form, stagnant in their ability to transform with the changing and evolving consciousness of humankind.

Just as our perception of words held the power to evolve our consciousness, in many ways, I felt travel perpetuated the evolution of our consciousness as well. How could it not do so when it exposed us to new worlds and new perspectives? For me, travel was the school of life, a Hogwarts for the expansion of my own worldview. And I was ever so curious to explore the depths of that worldview on a physical and spiritual plain.

That evening by the river, I watched my krathong glide gracefully along the midnight blanket of the Chao Phraya, passing by hundreds of candle-lit, lotus-shaped oblations sprinkled with the glitter of prayers and gratitude. Despite my immensely curious mind and desire to push the boundaries of it, I was glad to feel something that words, no matter the nature of their origins or the religions which claimed to concoct them, could clearly not explain. For there are some things that exist beyond the boundaries of consciousness, some secrets we are not meant to know.

Chapter 10 - Banana pancakes

I headed overland by bus through the central plains of Thailand and towards the south-eastern province of Trat. I was on my way to Koh Chang, one of Thailand's lesser-frequented isles, recommended to me as a balmy precursor to mainland Cambodia. Overland transportation was one method I adopted to keep my travels sustainable. I soon became rather fond of long bus rides across the continent. I birthed some of my best ideas on those bus journeys.

One 45-minute ferry ride from the mainland and one motorised tuk-tuk ride later, my feet stepped on the sandy shores of Lonely Beach, a backpacker's haven in the Gulf of Thailand. There was a primordial feel to that beachside town. I could tell it hadn't been corrupted like its neighbour Koh Samui. It remained unscathed, detached from the infamous Banana Pancake Trail frequented by sun-seekers dressed in elephant-print harem pants, Chang-branded tank-tops and crumby flip-flops.

Rustic bamboo shacks with palm-leaf roofs lined the narrow streets of Lonely Beach, fit only for tuk-tuks and scooters. Kaleidoscopic fruit stalls, presenting a smorgasbord of exotic, tropical fruits such as dragon fruit, mangosteen and longan, enticed passers-by. Thatched-roof beach huts scattered the coastline shaded by tall palm trees leaning over the ocean as if to summon a kiss from the waves. The distant sounds of reggae beats emitted from local venues posing as restaurants by day and bars by night, or bars by day depending on the mood of the patrons. It was hard to pass up a Chang beer at midday for 50 cents a glass. On Koh Chang, beer was cheaper than water.

On the ferry ride over, I'd befriended a group of travellers who befriended each other not too long before I had met them. An aspiring musician from California, a nursing student from Ireland and a free-spirited Brazilian woman who, like me, had traded her life in the corporate stockade for freedom and the chance to see the world. They immediately became my Koh Chang family.

Our first night out exploring Lonely Beach was unintentionally a Monday, the quietest night of the week in the town. Our Californian friend had barely started playing his ukulele when the dainty sounds echoing from his strings drew the attention of one of the local bar owners.

"Sawadee-kah," said a voice coming from a nearby dwelling. "Welcome to Banana Leaf. Will you join us?"

We followed his voice and entered the bar through a makeshift wooden archway that would have barely passed building safety standards. The contraption was irregularly hammered with rugged, hand-painted signs made of broken wood. The signs read the names of different countries from all over the world painted in various colours: Austria, Namibia, Malaysia, Argentina, Ukraine, Togo and many more. Despite the signs' imperfections, it made this meandering traveller feel rather welcome.

We sat in a cosy nook beneath the profile of Al Pacino on a black and white *Scarface* poster erected on the feeble walls of the venue and placed our sweating glasses of Chang down on a small wooden table. The owner of the bar, Dandy, took an instant liking to my friend's talent. He asked him if he wanted to be the night's entertainment and perform some of his own music. My friend gladly accepted and so we were gifted with his genuine performance.

On any other day, the bar featured musicians from all over the world. If a musician was absent, the floor was offered for open mic performances to those feeling like 15-minutes of fame. I recall sitting in that bar listening to the sweet sounds of the ukulele, a mirror ball reflected spots of green and pink across my face. I looked down and noticed the condensation of the glass soaking millimetre-by-

77

millimetre into the drink coaster atop the hand-carved wooden table in front of me. I was so present. Life had become so simple, and that simplicity soothed me the way gentle raindrops on my skin do. I had nowhere to be, nothing to attend to. I didn't even know what day of the week it was.

"Play 'Banana Pancakes'," I requested as the lyrics to Jack Johnson's melody sang through my mind.

It seemed only fitting to request that song as, earlier that day, I'd devoured the most delectable banana pancakes from a street vendor on Main street, cut into bite-sized squares and garnished with swivels of chocolate sauce.

Maybe we could sleep in
Make you banana pancakes
Pretend like it's the weekend, now
We could pretend it all the time

I didn't have to pretend. Life was no longer Monday to Friday for me. Banana pancakes were every day.

I spent the next few days lazing by the calming ocean waters, eating two-dollar pad thai and drinking one-dollar fruit shakes: some days mango, some days watermelon and some days papaya. I felt as though I could have spent months on that island without even noticing time go by, sinking into her like quicksand until she swallowed me whole and never let me go. But I knew I had to move on. My journey had just begun. I had to give in to the hands of time which, on that island, did not exist. And so, I continued, leaving only footprints in the sand and a heavy hope that Koh Chang would preserve her golden ambience and somehow, in a world wanting to primp her, maintain her unscathed natural beauty.

As Christmas approached that year, I found myself in a country very familiar to me. Cambodia had taken a piece of my heart on two separate occasions in the years prior. Once, when my friend Adam and I worked on an education project on the outskirts of Siem Reap, assisting in the construction of a classroom for marginalised children and youth. And again, when I returned to visit that project and deepened my relationship with the country and the people I had met there, including a young man from Portsmouth with whom I had an incredibly lustful romance. He came in and out of my life with the fleeting beauty of a shooting star.

However, this time I wasn't headed directly to Siem Reap – the gateway to the ancient temples of Angkor Wat. I was to travel overland to visit some of the more rural regions of Cambodia before spending Christmas in the capital city of Phnom Penh. I was intrigued by a community-based tourism project situated in the Cardamom Mountains, one of the few remaining forests located in western Cambodia. I decided that would be my first stop.

The project was located in the remote village of Chi Phat, about 25 kilometres outside the province of Andoung Tuek. To use the word remote was quite an understatement. Chi Phat was reachable only by motorbike on an unsealed dirt road or by a small riverboat down the Preak Piphot River.

I followed the instructions written on the Chi Phat tourism website which mentioned how to reach the isolated community. The instructions led me to the Kim Chhourn restaurant. I looked around curiously for the blue pillars mentioned in their guide, feeling as though I was a part of *The Amazing Race* looking for clues to help me progress forward in the game. Backpack in tow, I walked up to one of the men sitting near some parked motorbikes, a half-lit cigarette hung from the corner of his mouth.

"Chi Phat?" I asked.

"Yes," he responded, "Seven dollar."

That was the price mentioned on the tourism website. I didn't have to haggle or negotiate. Not that I would have. I was too fixated on safely getting to my destination.

The man straddled the motorbike, revved the ignition and prompted me to sit behind him. My backpack weighed almost a quarter of my body weight, so I had to activate my core muscles to not topple backwards like one of those inflatable waving tube men who fell with the wind. There was some stealth activation in those few minutes as the motorbike propelled down the red clay-earth road ahead. We drove beside tall fields of maize that stretched out beneath a patched, cloudy sky. The further we continued, the narrower the road became until we turned off and into the maize itself, down a path only as wide as the wheels of the motorbike. I could almost reach out and touch the walls of tall grass that confined us, but I dared not take my sweaty palms off the seat handles. I was mildly unnerved but mostly invigorated. My eyes were fixated on the clearing of grass ahead. Ah, a light at the end of the tunnel, I thought with relief.

We emerged from the maize and onto another dirt track that led to a denser area of forest. Through the glade, I glimpsed a sight of trees reflecting on water, which became clearer as the motorbike crept closer to its edge. We stopped in a nearby clearing of grass. A lone brown cow continued its lunch unbothered by the sound of our halting engine.

"*Au kun*," I said to the driver as I bowed my head and graciously acknowledged his service.

The language barrier between us was too strong to warrant any other dialogue but much can be said without words. I pulled seven one-dollar bills from my wallet and placed them into his tired hands. His umber eyes thanked me as he pointed in the direction of the river.

"Boat," he said.

There, at the riverbank, conjoined planks of wood lay on the shore creating a makeshift boat ramp to the water. A jagged-edged pontoon made of wooden planks, mostly broken, sat at the end of a frail walkway floating atop the navy creek. A gaunt Cambodian man wearing a droopy, military-camouflage, wide-brimmed hat stood barefoot on the pontoon, one hand on the attached rusted motor, and the other waving at me to summon my embarkment. He prompted me onto the rocky pontoon.

Beyond him, over the river and about 150 metres from where I stood, I could see the stilted houses of Chi Phat – the entrance to this concealed hamlet. The walls of the shanty homes reflected colours of azure blue, forest green and clay brown into the glassy river below, blurred by the waves dancing to the motion of our boat.

Chi Phat was an impoverished mountain community that, in 2007, was chosen to participate in an ecotourism project funded by the international non-profit forest and wildlife conservation organisation, Wildlife Alliance. The aim of the project was to encourage tourism in the region to create a more sustainable pathway for economic growth and halt pernicious means of income generation. Prior to the project's initiation, community members had little choice but to rely on illegal practices like tree-logging and poaching, as a way to earn money to provide for their families. Oftentimes, poverty was the underlying cause of forest destruction and wildlife poaching in remote communities like Chi Phat. That cause-and-effect echoed throughout the disposition of developing nations around the world, and during my travels, I would come across many ecotourism models like Chi Phat which had successfully influenced the cessation of forest and wildlife destruction within the communities they infiltrated.

Since the intervention of Wildlife Alliance in 2007, Chi Phat had welcomed over twelve thousand tourists. Some community members, who had previously found employment through forest logging, had now transformed their traditional Khmer homes into homestays, and welcomed guests as part of Chi Phat's fair-share accommodation scheme. Some community members now acted as guides for forest treks, while others served at the local restaurant. It was inspiring to see such opportunities for economic development generated by the sustainable tourism model. I wrote about this in my journalism and would continue to reference Chi Phat as a successful archetype for sustainable development in the years to come.

That evening in the village, as I lay in my homestay beneath a bright pink mosquito net canopy that protected me like a noble queen from the Middle Ages, I felt glad to make up a part of the statistic of travellers who'd ventured to Chi Phat to support such a project. And that night, somewhere deep within the rainforests of the Cardamom Mountains, I fell peacefully asleep to a lullaby sonnet of gibbon calls and cicada vibrations.

In December, I navigated the veins of the Kingdom of Cambodia, from vibrant, umbrella-spotted beaches in Sihanoukville, to permaculture farms and mangroves in the charming riverside town of Kampot. I spent a few nights deep in the lowland forests of Mondulkiri, in the country's east, where I visited an elephant sanctuary and learned about the plight of this endangered species, threatened by an increasing loss of natural habitat.

At the time I visited the sanctuary, the province of Mondulkiri was under immense threat from illegal forest logging. In October 2013, the non-profit organisation, Mondulkiri Project, signed an agreement with Bunong indigenous elders from the Putang Village to stop logging in an area of the forest near the provincial capital of Sen Monorom. This area became a sanctuary for four rescued elephants: Princess, Happy, Comvine and Sophie. I spent one day with the elephants as a part of the project's income generation experience for the local community. I watched them walk freely around the forest, eating any flora in their way to make up for the hefty dietary requirement of roughly 150 kilograms of foliage per day. I learned the history of their lives before the sanctuary; how the scars on Princess' back were from the days a large wooden seat carried the weight of tourists on so-called 'attractions'. At the time, it was common for elephants to be used in the tourism industry, but animal rights organisations soon caught on and were working tirelessly to bring this unethical treatment to the eyes of the mainstream population. However, the solution was not as simple as returning these magnificent creatures to the forests they came from because the forests were no longer there, destroyed by deforestation. So, the focus of many organisations like the Mondulkiri Project shifted to reforestation and the protection of the forests themselves.

I interviewed the Mondulkiri Project's appropriately named project founder, Mr Tree, in a 2015 interview.

He said, "Providing elephant and jungle trekking experiences and developing traditional medicines from the forests helps to generate income for the Bunong indigenous people. This can help to save habitats for elephants and other endangered wildlife and protect their future."

My visit to Mondulkiri exposed me, once again, to the reality of poverty in this world. Our world was divided between the haves and have nots, and that divide was not only prevalent in the Global South. I had witnessed poverty and inequality across cultures, from the sprawling downtown neighbourhoods of Los Angeles to the central districts of Manila, to the outback towns of Australia's Northern Territory. In all my work and all my observations, I had never solved what pieces of the equation were missing for us to live in a harmonious world where all people had their basic needs met: food, water, shelter, safety. Not I, nor any of the most influential people in the world, seemed to be able to solve that equation as far as history could tell. There was always somebody trying to get ahead of all the others – a king, a prince, a billionaire named Jeff. And we continued to exist this way, to benefit only those small few: the one percent. I didn't understand it really – the never-ending profit margins, the private jets, the Rolexes – but I sincerely hoped that one day we might find the $E = mc^2$ equivalent for global equality.

Cambodia's sluggish economic development was largely influenced by a sinister modern history. A sequence of oppressive regimes, a civil war and one of the worst genocides in the 20th century was the perfect storm to perpetuate poverty in the region. Flow-on effects such as lack of access to education, a shortage of skilled workers and a growing rural population, with little access to social security, slowed the growth of the country, until new economic pathways emerged through the tourism, agricultural and textiles sectors.

I was no economist, but learning about the relationship between history, poverty and the economy helped my mind to piece together their correlation. I always felt it important to learn about the intricacies of a destination before I travelled there: the history, the socio-economic circumstances, the plight of the population; especially, indigenous and marginalised communities. I seldom felt comfortable as an unread tourist visiting the top five attractions listed on Tripadvisor and jetting off.

Specifically, in Cambodia, I felt obliged to know of and acknowledge the genocide that happened there by the Khmer Rouge between 1975 and 1979. It is said that between 1.5 and 3 million souls were lost at the hands of the communist political group whose agenda was to create a classless agrarian society. While in Phnom Penh, I visited the harrowing Tuol Sleng Genocide Museum to learn more about this mammoth tragedy. Cold shivers ran down my spine as I saw the pictures of the faces of those innocent lives lost. I thought about all the friendly smiling Cambodians who had made me feel so welcome days prior, and how the victims in the pictures could have been their fathers, brothers, spouses. I wondered how long it would take for the pain of this atrocity to be washed away with the monsoon rains. My Auntie Frances used to say to me, "We should always learn about our history, so it is never repeated." I wished for that to be true.

I went to pay my respects at a memorial in Phnom Penh, erected to honour the victims. Rustic bamboo posts formed a fence around the grounds. In the centre, a young chartreuse lawn laid the base for the Choeung Ek Memorial Stupa, built with architecture similar to a Buddhist temple. It had a triangular roof, decorated with square tiles of yellow and teal, and intricate Khmer carvings. The white-painted concrete walls protected a glass tomb inside which held 6,426 sets of human bones found at this mass grave. 'The Killing Fields' is what most people referred to the site as. I preferred the name 'memorial'.

I looked out at the lawn, at the young grass. My mind transported me back to a time when I visited the Mount Batur volcano in Bali, Indonesia and saw grass growing from volcanic rock that was once lava. It reminded me there will always be rebirth, that life will go on even when the fierce fires of destruction blaze around us.

I walked towards the bamboo fence that lined the surrounding yard. As I approached it, I saw what resembled coloured decorations, but as I looked closer, I saw they were bracelets offered by the people; graciously placed over each post like thousands of circular horseshoes. At that moment, I loosened one of the bohemian stringed bracelets I had purchased from a street vendor in Thailand, gently pulled it from my wrist and placed it among the others. Tears welled in my eyes as I bowed my head.

Never forgotten.

Chapter 11 - Sliding doors

Christmas in Phnom Penh was different to any other Christmas I had experienced. I woke up with a ghastly hangover on the morning of 25 December at the Mad Monkey Hostel, located in the popular BKK1 district. I had travelled long enough to learn that hangovers and hostels were usually part and parcel.

The hostel bar had a bazuka shots tally board and marked each country with one point if they took a shot. The board read, "Before you leave, you have to take at least one. Do it for your country!" Naturally, I represented Australia that Christmas eve. Perhaps it was the most Australian element to my Christmas that year.

I had been on the road for less than a few months, yet my collection of experiences was growing immensely. I was connecting to people and to places, I was writing, and I was learning about incredible projects making waves in their respective causes and communities. I'd even had a few external publications pick up some of my freelance journalism pieces about sustainable tourism. It was a time when the world felt so new, like the way it would to a five-year-old. But five-year-olds miss their parents, and that Christmas, I started to exhibit some mild attachment anxiety. A looming loneliness sat beside me.

That morning, I conducted the rounds of Merry Christmas phone calls – Mum, Dad, auntie, uncle, sisters, friends, boyfriend. Conor and I had decided to try long-distance with the aim that he would visit me on parts of my journey. I thought it rather sweet of him to offer such an arrangement, having only known me for a short period of time. It just so happened that his father was living in Phuket at the time, and so we had arranged to meet up in early January for some travel around the southern region of Thailand. Knowing I would be seeing him and then my two friends, Ana and Amber, shortly after soothed some of the anxiety I was experiencing. The feelings of loneliness had caught me off-guard, though I had a mild inclination as to the roots of their origin. I hadn't really sat with the emotions brought upon by the drastic changes I had made to my life less than two months prior. I was too busy marvelling at the world around me. I didn't want to untangle that grief. I didn't want to feel uncomfortable. I wanted to feel invigorated. And so, I swept those feelings away like dust under a rug and continued to marvel, ignoring the messages from within.

The hostel restaurant was decorated with red placemats and holly-patterned Christmas crackers. Lunch was a Christmas roast with a selection of appropriately named festive cocktails – The Grinch, Christmas Cookie, Santa's Shots. I shuddered at the sight of the word 'shot' and strategically opted for a banana smoothie instead. My poisoned body was craving something cold on that thirty-degree afternoon. I was used to a warmer Christmas; I'd never known a Christmas in the winter. In Australia, Christmas meant summer barbeques in the backyard dressed in shorts and thongs (not the underwear kind, rather the Australian name for flip-flops), with a tinnie (can of beer) in one hand and a sanga (sausage sandwich) in the other, while the UV rays of the sun sept through our 50+ sunblock. We'd still leave milk and cookies out for Santa. Although, as a child, I'd often wonder how he'd fare in the Australian heat with that thick white beard and brumal attire.

The humidity of the air in Phnom Penh took me back to those Christmas days in Australia surrounded by friends and family, and as the faint sounds of the percussion to 'Jingle Bells' blended into distant chatter and white noise coming from the street, I sat among a table full of foreigners for a unique type of orphan's Christmas in Cambodia.

I was yet to revisit Siem Reap, a city that had become somewhat of a distant lover to me. There are places in this world that seduce you like lovers do. Siem Reap was one of those places. I would soon journey back into the arms of that distinguished epicentre to welcome in the new year, and to take a deep dive into the philanthropic soul that fed progress into that marvellous town.

What fascinated me the most about Siem Reap wasn't only its depth and vibrancy, but the innovation sprouting from its roots. Throughout my journalism at the time, I would actively seek out initiatives that were focused on offering solutions to social and environmental problems, with the aim to share those stories with the world. After some time and experience in this socially and environmentally conscious realm, it became clear to me there was a sweet spot for sustainable development to flourish. The variables of that sweet spot included a clear problem to be solved, a revenue stream, and a supportive community that were enabled to feel deeply connected to the cause itself, whether through storytelling or personal interaction. I felt Siem Reap encompassed those variables and was advantaged by the transient tourist population who walked the thoroughfare to visit the ancient temples of Angkor Wat.

In recent years, Siem Reap sprouted numerous businesses that embodied the social enterprise model. A social enterprise is a business whose objectives served a social mission. Unlike non-governmental organisations – who acquired funds through donations – social enterprises are able to acquire funds through business. For example, the sale of goods or services. Those funds can then be used to subsidise further development work or further the enterprise's social mission.

By the time I had spent a few days in Siem Reap, I had learned about many social enterprises. There was Haven café and New Leaf café, both training restaurants focused on providing valuable work experience and hospitality training to underprivileged young adults, who had left orphanages and safe shelters. There was Eco Soap Bank, a social enterprise that collected used soap bars from hotels to be sanitised and recycled into liquid soap and donated to schools, hospitals and humanitarian organisations working in disadvantaged communities. Their aim was to promote the importance of sanitation and ensure that communities remained safe from preventable illnesses while combating waste issues at the same time. My visit to the Eco Soap Bank headquarters and participation in a soap-making class was part of the revenue model they used to fund the impactful project.

Then there was Phare Circus, an organisation that promoted community development through the arts by offering education and sports scholarships to marginalised youth. Their revenue was brought about by ticket sales to the fantastic bi-nightly performances at the Phare Ponleu Selpak Circus, which maintained the #1 attraction in Siem Reap, an achievement which, at the time, was rare for a socially conscious initiative like Phare. And then there was the Blossom café, a piquant mirage for a sweet-tooth like me. The dainty café on Central Market Street was part of a small franchise of vocational training centres for vulnerable women in the community. Women were offered hospitality training in culinary and baking arts and would learn to construct the most impeccably decorated cakes and cupcakes I'd ever seen. The café was interiorly decorated with cyan blue table covers, cushioned chairs, and sofas with red and white polka-dot cushions atop them. The walls were white to contrast the vivid colours of the décor, and to exacerbate the marvellous cakes displayed on the shelves on those walls. I would spend many afternoons at that café, writing on my laptop, sipping on a hot chocolate and intermittently biting into a perfectly prepared cupcake – either Red Velvet, the colour of the cushions themselves, with an off-white swirl of icing on the top and sprinkled with edible silver pearls, or a rich, dark chocolate and salted caramel number which spoke to my taste buds the way Siem Reap spoke to my heart.

To be surrounded by that type of social innovation inspired me immensely. Whenever the incessant, distressing global news entered my sphere of attention, I would turn my focus to the compassionate, solutions-oriented people who powered those enterprises – the ones who showed up to the world and said, "I am here to help you." They gave me hope.

One morning before the year came to an end, I woke up before sunrise to visit the Angkor Wat temples at dawn. I always felt there to be something quite remarkable about the early mornings. It was a time for awakening after rest, an opportunity to start anew. Whenever a challenging day came to an end, I would humbly whisper to myself, "Everything will be better in the morning," and more often than not, it was. I wondered if my love for the dawn derived from the fact I was born at exactly five minutes past six o'clock in the morning. As Earth entered its chancy bi-annual encounter with the Torrid Meteor stream and the sun shone its light over the Pacific Ocean that frosty morning of 30 June, I opened my eyes to the light of my new world. Unsuspecting that potentially thirty-six thousand mornings lay ahead of me, thirty-six thousand dawns to start anew.

Angkor Wat at sunrise offered a spectacular panorama. The first daylight peered through a sky blending hues of blue and violet, like watercolour brush strokes on canvas. A small crowd gathered by the left side of the walkway to the temples, beyond a reflection pond which created a striking mirror image of the temples and the sky. Under their morning shadow, the five distinct stone towers befittingly resembled mountain tops. Records suggest the towers were intended to mimic the five mountain ranges of Mt Meru – the mythical home of the gods.

The 12th-century temples had long been a place of worship, originally for Hindus and then Buddhists. In modern times, they stood as Cambodia's top tourist attraction, although turmeric-robed Buddhist monks still frequented the area offering prayers and reverence.

As the sun rose up behind the temples, a lightening shadow unveiled the stone carvings on their walls. I walked closer to the structure, admiring the grey sandstone murals. As I touched the cold stone, I imagined who had touched this stone before me. *Who erected this stone? What was life like for them? What did they believe in?*

I had read about the temple's alignment with the sun – how on the spring equinox, when night and day are of equal length, the rising sun lines directly with the central tower. This led me to believe that there was indeed careful precision placed on the architecture and alignment of this ancient wonder, similarly to that of Chichén Itzá, Mexico and Ħaġar Qim in Malta. Perhaps those people knew more about our connection to the cosmos than we do in modern times.

There was magical energy to that ancient wonder. My curiosity put my mind in a time machine and spit me out in a bygone century. I walked through the temples in wonderment, imagining the ways in which the people of that civilisation lived and how they communicated with one another. I wondered if life was easier for them, or if life was harder. *Did they face the same struggles as we do today? Was there a hierarchy in their societies? Were there inequalities? Were women treated well?*

Oftentimes, ancient history wouldn't provide these answers. Mostly, because there was much knowledge lost over time but also, because the industry itself came with the baggage of bureaucracy. I'd rarely let myself subscribe to a specific hypothesis when it came to ancient history. Instead, I liked to ask the questions that had no answers and let my imagination run wild with the could-have-been and the visions of a utopia that existed once upon a time.

I saw in the year that was from a rowdy Pub Street – a central street in Siem Reap that housed all the town's main late-night venues. It was similar to Bangkok's infamous Khao San Road – a place where anything goes and things could get as weird as Willy Wonka's Chocolate Factory except, instead of gum that turned you into an enormous blueberry, you'd find edible deep-fried grasshoppers and tarantulas, snakes on skewers, and spit-roast frogs. I was accompanied by three other backpackers from my hostel. In our glamorous attire of flip-flops, shorts and tees, we danced in the streets to music blaring from the overcrowded venues. I noticed we were near a venue familiar to me. The recognisable fluorescent painted walls of Angkor What? Bar reflected ultraviolet lights and the colours shone out to the street. My minds-eye accessed the memories of nights I'd danced on those table-tops without a care in the world, painted in the kinds of liberating fluorescent colours that complemented the walls. I peered inside, looking for the face of a person I once knew. They were no longer there. The sliding doors of that train had closed.

There's a kind of serendipity that surrounds how easily our lives can change course if we miss one train or if we are late for the bus – if we take the left turn or the right turn. Every moment we encounter with someone could be a moment that changes our lives. Every decision we make throughout our entire existence could be the decision that influences the course of our life from that moment forth.

I had made a lot of big decisions that year, and as I danced in Pub Street that evening of 31 December, the train to a new year approached my station.

Chapter 12 - Conor

"Would you like a snack?" the air hostess asked.

Her muted words blended with the lyrics of 'Don't Ever' by Missy Higgins sounding through my cabled headphones. I removed one of the earbuds and made eye contact, to assure her I did hear the prompt.

"Sure," I replied, eyeing a packet of what looked to be Oreos in her hands.

"Actually, on second thought, no thank you," I said as the irony sank in that those Oreos contained the same palm oil that was linked to forest destruction and human right abuses in Malaysia and Indonesia.

I was on my way to Phuket, Thailand, to spend some weeks on a hiatus from my hiatus. I was beginning to sense there was a form of exhaustion that accompanied long-term travel. It felt as though my travels were beginning to resemble a long-distance run whereby, although there were pit stops and water stations along the way, the longer I ran, the wearier I became. The surprise of a new destination gave me a similar hit to an isotonic sports drink, but the zeal soon wore off. The taste of an exotic, foreign dish gave me the same energy as a protein bar but soon became commonplace. It seemed all my body really wanted was to stop in its tracks.

The mountains of Phang-Nga distracted me. I marvelled at their pine beauty as we descended into Phuket. I was nervous. It had been over two months since I had seen Conor, two months since I left that world behind. I wondered how this week would shape us as a couple. We had never travelled together. In the grand scheme of things, our relationship was immature, but I was excited to see him, nonetheless.

I carried my distinct 13-kilogram orange backpack down the airstairs and onto the tarmac headed for the terminal. I thought it best to stop by the restrooms to check how I looked for our anticipated reunion. If I was flaunting a fashion statement, it would be 'backpacker'. I had become an elephant-printed, bohemian-accessorised mannequin. My hair had grown to the length of my elbows, my eyebrows hadn't been trimmed in months and being a traveller had stripped from me the desire to wear any makeup at all. That was simply too much maintenance for the transient lifestyle I had adopted.

I stood in the women's restroom and looked over the hand basin into the mirror. The combination of a soft tan and eighty percent humidity gave my skin the kind of glow that resembled a tinted moisturiser. I thought to open my bag and take out my mascara but the more I looked at the natural girl in the mirror, her carob brown eyes and freckled lips staring back at me, the fonder I became of her.

I had been painted and moulded since age thirteen. Since the boy I had a crush on told me I was too ugly. Since I got teased in high school for not wearing a bra and I was told my legs were too hairy. I only had thirteen years of this life before I was compelled to change the way I looked in order to fit in. That's about two years more than girls in the modern day, exposed to a plethora of unrealistic beauty standards. From what I recall, The Spice Girls maintained a more realistic level of beauty than the Kardashians. I don't remember looking at Sporty Spice and feeling as though I needed butt injections.

Once I began wearing makeup at a young age, I started to dislike the way I looked without it. Throughout my late teen years and into my mid-twenties, I wouldn't even leave the house without wearing mascara. I felt ugly without it. *But ugly to who? Who was I trying to impress?* With hindsight, I was hiding. Camouflaged in the paint of insecurity. I walked in a world that judged all facets of my being, and the more I felt judged, the more insecure I became until I lost almost all of my confidence and was left to mine for the pieces of my own self-love like '49ers in the Gold Rush.

It seemed in much of our societal dispositions, no matter what continent you came from, people were obsessively invested in the way women dressed, spoke, spent their time and lived their lives. We were ceaselessly governed, in spoken and unspoken ways. And the governance was so deeply rooted, it even manifested from within our own sisterhoods. We were weighed down, us women. The discrimination, the judgement, the censorship, the inequality. It left us fighting an uphill battle for true freedom and autonomy, but shimmers of matriarchal light shone through those clouds on dark days.

I was fortunate enough to have learned to commence the removal of much of the lint stuck to my being from the tumble dry of archaic patriarchal governance I spent the majority of my life living among. But it was still there, each piece of lint a censorious smirk, a condescending comment. An impudent insult, a self-deprecating thought. Ridding myself of more than ten years of self-deprecation was not an unchallenging feat. Although, I felt the sheer act of removing myself from being subjected to the passive judgement that simmered in perpetual societies helped this transition.

I walked down the hallway, past the baggage claim and towards the exit sign to Phuket's International airport. My heart was beating rapidly, eager to see Conor's face, to be held in the arms of someone again. My eyes scanned the crowd of people waiting to greet their friends, family members and loved ones. There was a special energy to arrival terminals. They were a lodestone for all the emotions that existed in love's manifestation.

I continued to scan the faces of the people, waiting for my neurons to signal a person familiar. And then, among the sea of unfamiliar eyes, I saw him; that warming essence lighting up the room. He was walking right towards me, dressed in true backpacker attire – an indigo tank top, cargo shorts and thongs, a rucksack on his shoulders and a black leather-stringed necklace holding a sterling silver gecko pendant.

My legs sped up and I paced toward him. The closer we got to each other, the bigger our smiles grew until we were close enough for our smiling lips to touch.

"It's so good to see you!" he said as he held me close, squeezing me tightly in one of his comforting hugs. Conor was one of those people who hugged you like a Southern European uncle would. His hugs were a true act of endearment.

"You too!" I replied.

"You look great!" he said, his compliment making me blush.

"You do too. You had a haircut." I smiled.

His shorter hair and trimmed beard made him look younger than he did when we met. He looked a little less like the hipster bartender I met in the inner-west and more like a vacationing undergrad, but he had the same aura. It was warm, and his soft, embracing arms comforted me like they had done all those months before.

"Dad is on the way to pick us up and then we'll head to the hotel," he said.

We had planned to spend a few days chaperoned by Conor's father who lived a few months of the year in his condo near Phuket. Then, we would drive north to the beachside villages of Khao Lak and continue exploring the luscious rainforests and inland lakes of the Khao Sok National Park. Thailand was often famed for its beaches, but the country also flaunted 102 national parks and some of the oldest evergreen forests in the world, including Khao Sok which covered a whole 739 square kilometres of Thailand's Surat Thani province.

Over the following days, we drove along the Andaman Sea coastline, stopping at secluded beaches and hidden waterfalls. We were utterly encompassed by nature. Conor's father had told us about a serene and secluded emerald lake enclosed by prehistoric limestone rock formations and tropical rainforests where visitors could sleep in rustic lake houses, and wake upon the emerald blanket of the lake itself. Conor and I decided to spend some days there and so created a modern-day treasure map to endeavour to reach the sequestered destination. Conveniently, much of Thailand had reliable bus routes and so we found directions to a local accommodation base where we would then be able to book an onward journey to the lake.

Our bus dropped us in the heart of Khao Sok National Park. One main thoroughfare housed the majority of the guesthouses in the park, but the rest of the land was untouched. A fierce forest engulfed us in all directions and her welcomed music rang through our ears as we gathered our bearings.

"I think this is the place," I said to Conor as I navigated the compass that was Google Maps and pointed towards a sign that read Monkey Mansion Jungalows.

We approached the reception desk that sat in an open-plan, contemporary Thai wooden building. Colourful hammocks hung from the roof slabs, Thai cushions lined the floors beneath carved wooden tables. A golden labrador sat, legs sprawled, cooling beneath the ceiling fan. My interest was piqued when I saw the words 'avoid plastic' hand-painted on a piece of driftwood near the entrance to the path that led to the bungalows. These people were speaking my language.

"It's beautiful here," Conor said, his eyes twinkling with the beauty of Thailand.

It made me happy to watch him in reverence. In the few days we had been together, I observed the weight of Sydney evaporate off him and disappear into the forests like carbon. Although Sydney was a relatively small city in comparison to the likes of New York or London, there was haste in its undertone.

If Sydney had a stereotypical persona, it would be the emotionally suppressed, stylish but edgy, white-collar worker who found life incredibly demanding yet engaged in the occasional debauchery on the weekends as an act of insensible escapism from those demands. People worked hard in Sydney. You had to. The cost of living was high and inflation rates were high. If you wanted to live a reasonably comfortable life you had to work at least forty hours per week, often in a job you didn't enjoy.

While Conor didn't exactly fit that stereotype, with his bartending stints and on-the-side passion projects, I felt the energies of the city still weighed him down. That week in Thailand distanced him from those insisting pressures and constant stimulation. I could sense the freedom and stillness were intoxicating him, the way it would for an inmate in a rec yard staring at the azure sky as if for the first time.

The Monkey Mansion Jungalows consisted of a series of simple, arcadian bungalows with triangular tin roofs and railings that looked like tree trunks. Each cabin was encircled by dipterocarp and banana trees, and had its own small garden of tropical plants along an earth path that led to the common area. The rooms were fitted with wooden furnishings, their colours rooted in nature.

We spent the evening there organising our plans to get to Cheow Lan Lake. The guesthouse offered overnight lake tours and so we organised one for the following day. Pick-up was at 9 am in order to allow enough time to reach the pier for our onwards long-tail boat ride through the lake and to the floating bungalows.

That journey upon Cheow Lan Lake was one of the most spectacular experiences I had ever encountered. Our traditional long-tail boat glided through the smaragdine waters of an enclosed paradise and towards primitive bamboo bungalows that sat in a line atop wooden planks on the lake waters. We were surrounded by 360-degree views of the forests and mammoth limestone pillars, hundreds of metres tall. I'd never seen anything quite like it. As we disembarked the boat, we were handed the keys to our bungalow. Conor and I walked along the rickety bridge to find our allocated room. There were about twenty bungalows, floating side by side, atop buoyant branches and bamboo sticks. Beneath us were the clear depths of the lake. We were literally sleeping on water.

"This is incredible," Conor said to me as he navigated the walkway to our room.

The small shack consisted of one double mattress with bedding, a medium-sized fan attached to the side wall and a small globe that offered solar-powered electricity at certain periods of the day. We were the most juxtaposed contrast to inner Sydney living that we could possibly be.

We unpacked our bags. The barking of hornbills echoed through the trees as I looked out through the small rectangular opening of the bungalow door to forest ranges and inviting waters. Conor stood at the water's edge, admiring the enchanting lake before us. He turned his face towards me and smiled. Then, he dived off the walkway and into the heart of the lake, making an almost splashless entrance into her waters.

I undressed down to my bathing suit, tossing my clothes into the sparse area at the foot of the floored mattress. I hunched through the doorway and took a few steps to the edge of the platform.

"Are you coming in?" he said as he treaded the water below.

"Is it cold?" I replied.

"You'll see when you join me," he said, with a suggestive smile.

I gently placed one toe in the water to sense the temperature. It wasn't too cold and even if it was, I would have gone in. When would I have ever imagined experiencing such primitive beauty in all its rawness? And to experience it with someone I deeply admired? I would savour every minute.

I dived in, feeling through the water like silk bed sheets, my eyes open to witness it all. I emerged metres away from Conor. He swam up to me and placed a soft kiss on my lips.

"How beautiful is this?" he said.

"Just magical," I replied, in awe of everything around me.

We floated there for a moment, in each other's presence; earth and water intertwined.

"You've created a beautiful life for yourself, you know?" he said, his water-soaked skin glistening beneath the sun. "You make me feel like anything is possible in life."

"Anything *is* possible," I replied with enthusiasm, treading the water below me like riding an invisible, underwater bicycle. "I didn't realise it before, but I do now. If I'd never listened to my heart last year and left my career, if I never followed what felt true to me, I wouldn't be here right now. I guess I always felt there was another way to live this life."

"I'm glad you're here," he said. "I'm glad we're here together."

That evening, the lights went out at nine pm and the only light we had was from the torches on our phones or the stars that shone above the thatched roof of our bungalow. We lay side by side in the darkness, listening to the swooshing sounds of tiny waves and the distant calls of the forest's fauna.

"What will happen after this week?" I asked, eager to learn when I'd be able to see him again.

Conor was planning to go back to Australia, and I had another six months of travel ahead of me, potentially more. I was hesitant to ask the question, but I felt it was important to discuss *us*.

"I've been thinking about that too," he said. "I am going to try and come back for you. I love being here with you."

His words flattered me, and butterflies ran rampant around my stomach. It meant a lot to me to hear his thoughts out loud. It offered some foundation for the non-conventional, undetermined characterisation of our relationship at the time. I felt excited at the possibility that I could live this free-spirited existence and have someone I cared for by my side. Perhaps I really could have the fairytale love story, I thought to myself.

I fell asleep as a romantic dreamer that night, fizzy from all the experiences of the day gone by. But my dreams told a different tale. My subconscious took me away from the lake, through a hidden door and into a concealed chamber of my soul.

I was transported to an unfamiliar house. Dean was there. We were arguing. He had stormed out and I was angry and sad that he left me. *He must have moved on. I suppose I should too.*

In the next scene of my night play, a lady approached me. She told me a litter of puppies had been born and I had to follow her. In the play, time had passed since the argument between Dean and me. It had been a long time since I'd heard from him. I followed the lady. We approached a small room. I could hear the puppies inside. The lady prompted me to follow her as she entered a large grey door. I entered the room and was shocked to see Dean. He was tied to a chair as if he had been kidnapped. I ran over to him and attempted to rescue him. "I wanted to find you, but I didn't have a choice," he said.

"It's OK," I replied. "You're here now. You're safe ..."

My eyes shot open. I'd teleported from my night play and found myself back on Cheow Lan Lake, confined by the walls of the bungalow. For a brief moment, I lost my bearings. It wasn't until I looked beside me and saw Conor, peacefully asleep, his hand draped over me, that I realised where I was.

The dream left me unsettled for at least 30 minutes. I stared into the darkness, attempting to discern between my realities. It's just a dream, I thought to myself. *Go back to sleep.*

Since I could remember, I'd always had vivid dreams and I was often able to recollect them. Occasionally, before I would lay my head to rest, I'd joke about visiting this alternate universe in my sleep. Sometimes, this universe was a sci-fi movie so detailed and anomalous it could have been directed by James Cameron himself. Other times, parts of the dream would correlate to my everyday life, although the scenes were still as peculiar as Lewis Carroll might imagine. I liked to decipher them though, to see if they related to any parts of me, concealed or unconcealed. I feel all of us have concealed parts of ourselves, chambers that exist within us. The contents of those chambers may vary and change over time, but there is a depth to us that can often only be explored by connecting with the subconscious levels of our minds. Dreams are one pathway to connect to those contents, but only if and when we are ready to acknowledge they exist.

I woke the next day to morning light peeking through the space between the door and the woven walls of the bungalow. The calm movements of the water below us suppressed the silence of dawn and

I found my way back to presence, back to my exquisite reality. I leaned over and placed a kiss on Conor's cheek.

"I'm going to go for a quick morning swim," I whispered in his ear.

"No worries," he said in a muffled early-morning tone. "I'll sleep a little longer."

I sat on the dock with my feet in the emerald waters of the lake. I stared down at them, beneath the transparent water, and caught the muddled ripples of my own reflection. Visions of the dream reappeared in my mind's eye, but I attempted to snuff them away.

There was not a person in sight that morning, just me, a faint dawn chorus of songbirds and the sound of the forest's wisdom.

"All is as it is intended to be, Bianca. Be here now," she whispered.

Chapter 13 - Farm to table

The start of my year was nourishing. After those weeks in southern Thailand with Conor and in northern Thailand with my two zest-for-life, fellow-city-folk-turned-adventurers, Ana and Amber, I felt nurtured. The feeling of being in the presence of someone who knows you well is comforting. It's the space you long for when the day has grown weary. It's the flame that ignites your spark when it is dim. I felt re-energised after being in their presence. They were my medicine, my sustenance for the road ahead.

Northern Thailand's city of Chiang Mai was an ideal thoroughfare to my next destination, which was Laos. Instead of taking a flight or bus, I opted for a more sustainable, albeit slower, mode of transportation – the slow boat.

The journey from Huay Xai to Luang Prabang on the Upper Mekong offered one of the last thriving boat fleets to the tourist trade in that region. Tourists could take a two-day or three-day journey on a traditional wooden slow boat down the vena cava of Asia, stopping at the small village of Pakbeng to meet the cordial hospitality of the local Hmong and Tai tribes, and then continuing on to Luang Prabang, one of Laos' prettiest destinations. Luang Prabang was given UNESCO World Heritage status in 1995, largely due to the distinctive architectural coalescence of both traditional Laotian temples and French Colonial manors that lined the streets and decorated the riverside.

I passed through customs on the Thai/Laos border. The customs office was a medium-sized shed with two men behind the counter, stamping passports as tourists passed through one by one. There was a small crowd of tourists but not too many to cause a delay. Their arbitrary attire and Patagonia backpacks made me feel as though they weren't the kind of people who would opt for the Deluxe Package at the Sheraton. They must have been there for the experience, or the fact it was the most economically viable option to get to Luang Prabang from our geographic location. I had heard down the grapevine that the slow boats weren't the most comfortable, with their seats about as intolerable as sitting on a wooden church pew for hours on end, but the experience still rated higher than a fifteen-hour zigzagging overnight bus journey in the darkness.

Roughly four or five long boats sat at the water's edge, floating atop the brown, murky waters of the Mekong. From afar, they looked like small wooden train carriages with open windows, their walls painted in lime green or sky-blue colours. As I approached the shore, I manoeuvred my way across a feeble wooden plank and into the boat. A man standing on the stern reached out his hand to offer me some extra balance. I lowered my head to fit through the small entrance where I was surprised, and relieved, to see some cushioning on the wooden chairs that symmetrically lined the boat's interior.

I seized the opportune moment to take a window seat. Window seats were always my favourite. The whooshing sounds of the Mekong instantly calmed me as I waited for the boat to fill. A young man sat next to me, greeting me with a smile.

"Hi, I'm Al," he said as he reached out his hand.

"I'm Bianca," I replied, reciprocating his gesture.

I admired the universal gesture of a handshake in my culture. Some theories on the origins of this action said the handshake began as a gesture of peace. Grasping hands proved you were not holding a weapon and therefore signalled a peaceful interaction. Whether that theory was true or not, I was appreciative when a stranger greeted me in that way. Specifically, when it manifested into a connection like the one Al and I had. He soon became my friend, and we spent some days travelling together through Laos.

As much as I enjoyed travelling alone, there were benefits to teaming up with a travel buddy every now and then. You could split costs, share rooms, lean on one another for support and, evidently, have someone to talk to on long boat journeys on the Mekong. Although I enjoyed the act of staring out the window at my surroundings for hours on end – letting my imagination run rampant and my thoughts take turns down unnamed streets – I did like to break up that daydreaming with some time in the present world and connect with other travellers who had their own wisdom to share.

Luang Prabang was as beautiful as they had mentioned in the Lonely Planet guidebooks and the online blogs. The town sat beneath the mountain ranges of PhouThao and PhouNang in a peninsula formed by the Mekong and the Nam Khan River. Oriental pagodas (vats) scattered among broadleaf forests. Traditional wooden terraces lined the quiet streets. During the early mornings, visitors could observe the local Theravada Buddhist monks receiving their morning alms. Occasionally, you'd catch their bright orange robes from the corner of your eye.

I distinctly recall a breakfast I consumed beneath the walnut wooden walls of a sidewalk café in the town centre called KopNoi. The combined café, art gallery and fair trade store worked closely with artisans and villagers in the community to procure and sell locally produced products as a way to promote and preserve traditional Laotian art heritage. Their homemade peanut butter, made with ground nuts grown in the rich soils of Luang Prabang, was the most delicious peanut butter I had ever tasted. It had a Nutella-like texture that draped like satin with every spread of the knife and smelled the way it would if I'd had my nose in a whole jar of the stuff. I had a Winnie the Pooh moment in that café. There is something about those remarkable moments we have with food. They imprint in our minds the same way our most tantalising sexual encounters do. Some say that good food ignites similar neural pathways to good sex. And like good sex, those seductive moments with food tend to appear when you least expect them. Like the time I found the most scrumptious chocolate cake at a small Indian restaurant in the middle of Jaipur. Or the time my sister and I discovered the best hotdogs we'd ever tasted at one of the small, green-coloured mini pavilions in the Tuileries Garden of Paris. Or the time I drank the most divine hot chocolate from a cafeteria in Sintra, Portugal. The Portuguese make a fine hot chocolate, if I do say so myself.

I spent a few more days in Luang Prabang, learning about a country I hadn't known much about prior to my visit there. I visited the Traditional Arts and Ethnology Centre, a museum dedicated to educating people about Laos' diverse culture and ethnic groups, as well as preserving its history. I learned there are more than 100 known ethnic groups in Laos, many of which have their own unique dialects and customs.

I visited the UXO Laos Visitor Centre, where I learned about the remnants of the Vietnam war and how unexploded bombs and mines still exist on the land, buried beneath and above the soil. I was saddened to hear how many unexploded ordinances still exist in Laos, claiming people's lives to this day. In 1996, the Laos National Unexploded Ordinance Program was established, attempting to rid the country of unexploded bombs and mines. But with over 270 million bombs dropped on the country between 1964 to 1973, and roughly 80 million of them unexploded, their goal was a mammoth assignment. There was some hope in sight though, with organisations like The Mines Advisory Group and the APOPO Hero Rats aiding this mission.

By the time February came to an end, I rode the currents of the Mekong like an Irrawaddy dolphin. I traversed south through the valleys of Vang Vieng, into the capital city of Vientiane and then further towards the edge of the Laos/Cambodian border. I was invited to the Bolaven Plateau, a region rife with coffee plantations sustained by the prevalence of the rich, high-altitude lava soil of an ancient, inactive volcano. I was there to share the story of Mr Khamsone and his venture, Mystic Mountain Coffee.

Mr Khamsone was a champion for protecting the livelihoods and rights of coffee growers in the region. He did this by advocating for fairer wages and sourcing international markets for the high-quality coffee of the Bolaven Plateau. I first learned about him while sitting in the Kinyei Café in Cambodia's Battambang and noticing a sign that read, 'We Sell Feel Good Coffee'. I investigated where that coffee had been sourced and learned about Mr Khamsone and his ecotourism initiative.

Mr Khamsone was researching the ways ecotourism and agro-tourism could offer alternate economic pathways for some of the more marginalised people that resided there, many of whom fell victim to the common exploitations found in supply chains like coffee.

I had, for many years, been deeply curious about the concept of fair trade and workers' rights. Not only in the food industry but in fashion and other consumer-driven trades. The more hands in the pie of a supply chain, the more exploitation seemed to occur. And the people at the start of that chain – the growers, the seamstresses, the farmers – were the ones exploited most, receiving the very last piece of that pie, or in many cases, a few meagre crumbs.

There were roughly 5000 families in the Paksong district whose income relied on the demand for coffee. Some were farmers, others were sorters and packers, and some traders, like Mr Khamsone. The harvest season for coffee usually began in November and ended in February, so we had arrived just in time to see some of the harvesting processes. It was evident the coffee many of us enjoyed each day had taken a long journey to get from the farm to our cups. Firstly, the fruits (also known as coffee cherries) were stripped off of the branches of the crops, often by hand. Then, the cherries were dried, graded and sorted to remove beans with colour flaws or other imperfections. And then, the milled beans were packed into either jute or sisal bags and shipped away for roasting. I witnessed the majority of the steps of that process in late February, and subsequently titled my story, 'There are people behind your coffee, and they're not the baristas'.

Mr Khamsone guided me to the home of one of the farmers. Large sheets of mesh were laid out on the front grounds of the home, acting as a base for the beans. A man raked them into an even layer. From afar, they looked like clumps of dark soil covering the ground, but up close you could see the thousands of tiny beans, moss-coloured in their immaturity.

A woman sat beneath the shade on the front verandah of the stilted wooden home. It was a warm day, and the dry air was filled with dust particles from the dirt road that the property stood upon. The home was simply constructed using wooden planks hammered together, and corrugated iron sheets to cover any open crannies. The region was significantly underdeveloped.

"Here you can see how the berries are sorted," Mr Khamsone explained.

The woman was sorting coffee beans with her bare hands, segmenting them into two piles of 'good-enough-for-roasting' and 'imperfections.' It would take one woman an average of three days to manually sort a 50-kilogram bag of coffee, for which she would receive an income based on the amount of coffee she sorted rather than the time it took to sort. On one hand, it was advantageous for women to work from home and be able to care for their families at the same time. However, on the other hand, the wages they earned were far from sufficient in comparison to the amount of money earned by the traders or the sellers. For one 50-kilogram bag of coffee sorted, a woman could earn as little as US$10 – the crumbs of the pie.

Mr Khamsone continued to share the challenges faced by the community there: how the farmers exist at the mercy of the weather, how they rely on the demand for coffee from Laos and other areas, and how they often fall victim to rising inflation rates. To be a farmer is a challenging occupation and those challenges are rarely acknowledged by the silent majority. There is a vast divide between the people of Paksong and those who obliviously brew their espresso in hundred-dollar coffee machines on Sunday mornings. Our society is far removed from the people behind our coffee, but the prevalence of fair trade is increasing.

That evening, I shared a meal with Mr Khamsone and his family in their family home, which he had transformed into a homestay for guests. It was a rather established stilted home on the outskirts of the plantation, on a small open plot of land surrounded by shrubs. We were joined by his wife and young daughter, who allowed me to join her in the colouring of her picture book.

Mr Khamsone's wife prepared us a family feast with sticky rice as the staple course. Sticky rice is very common in Laos. It is made using long grain rice cooked until glutinous and sticky and is often served in a bamboo basket, so the rice does not harden. It paired well with the *laap* I was served – a salad of meat and fresh herbs like mint and green onions. It also complemented the bowl of *or lam* – a spicy vegetable broth so hot it put my tear ducts into overdrive. I didn't have the audacity to ask for the mild version. I figured I could handle it.

The next morning, I woke to the intense sounds of a rooster's crow. *Who needs an alarm clock when you have a rooster?* Those cock-a-doodle-doos can be heard a mile away. My eyes squinted at the presence of daylight on a not-so-ordinary morning. I woke with the kind of belly pain that signified a rough day ahead. Either the capsaicin or some bacteria had caused an SOS in my digestive tract and struck me down. Not today, I thought. *Not here.*

In all my years of travel, I'd managed to avoid the dreaded "Delhi belly," "Bali belly" and any other kind of "belly" they appropriately brand the consequence of novice white folk who take their chances on some foreign dish, only to end up hugging the porcelain if they are so lucky as to find one. That bacteria must have gone into stealth mode to break through the force field of my self-proclaimed "stomach of steel." But they did. All systems were compromised.

I spent the next few days with little energy. Mr Khamsone and his wife were so kind as to let me rest in their home until I was well enough to continue on my journey and once again able to stomach a plate of sticky rice. What happened in the days after was a mental repercussion of those physically difficult hours. I was alone, far from the comfort of anything familiar. Far from friends. Far from family. I was far from the conventional comforts I had become so accustomed to over a life in a privileged country: a hot shower with avid water pressure, a Western toilet, a television, a food delivery service. And for the first time in a long while, I wanted to go back to Sydney. I wanted to click my ruby shoes together three times and get on the next flight out.

I called my mother.

"Hi honey," she answered.

"Hey, Mum," I replied.

"How are you? How is it all going?" she said.

"Not too great," I replied, my voice starting to tremble, awaiting the eruption of my tears like the dormant volcano beneath my feet.

I proceeded to fill Mum in on all that had been happening. I expressed my longing for familiarity. I told her about my bacteria invasion. She laughed a little, but mostly consoled me. My mother, father, sister and I have a very similar sense of humour and it was rare we wouldn't turn any situation into something to smile about.

"Try to find something that will bring you a little bit of joy," she said. "And if that doesn't help, you always have the choice to come home if you want."

The cognitive dissonance in my mind was powerful during those days in Laos. A part of me wanted to return to Sydney, although I knew my journey was far from over. Another part of me felt that if I returned to Sydney I would have failed in some way, that all I had given up to be there – specifically my relationship with Dean – would have been in vain. I wondered what I would return to. *What was there for me?* Even the thought of calling Sydney 'home' was foreign. It didn't feel like home anymore, a piece of my identity puzzle dissolving as each day went on.

The thoughts sent me further spiralling down a dark hallway of my own consciousness. *How powerful our minds are when we lose control of them, like a wild horse with no reins.* I needed something to distract me, to take my mind off the incessant discomfort it was causing itself. So, I turned to one of the most distracting inventions of the 21st century – Netflix.

I spent my last days in Laos watching reruns of *New Girl* at a hostel in the river town of Pakse. The earnest goofiness of Winston Bishop and the oddly relatable shenanigans of Jessica Day triggered just enough endorphins to keep me afloat that week.

Conor had been checking in on me to see how I was faring. We'd been discussing the logistics of him joining me in April. I was excited at the possibility of this, but also protecting myself. I wondered if he would change his mind and I'd be left feeling abandoned again. A part of me knew I was still wounded from my envisioned love-story manuscript that never made it to production. But then again, many of our manuscripts don't. I was learning that life was less like a fairytale and more like a never-ending rollercoaster where one moment you're shouting 'yippee' and then next you're muttering 'holy fuck'. And when the rollercoaster is descending, we are often challenged to let go of the way we imagine our lives will unfold, allowing those dreams and visions to fly away with the winds like the pappus of dandelions.

Chapter 14 - 7000 islands

In April, life's rollercoaster ascended, and Conor joined me on my travels, just as he had promised. We flew from Sydney to the Philippines together after I visited Australia that Easter. Thankfully, Sydney was an aviational stone's-throw away from Asia, and so the flights were relatively short in comparison to a round-the-world route.

The islands of the Philippines are located on Southeast Asia's eastern rim. The country consists of more than 7000 islands spread out over the South China Sea, the Sulu and Celebes Seas, and the Pacific Ocean. We chose that destination to start with due to the fact April was one of the last months of the dry season before monsoon rains arrived, and the risk of typhoons increased.

Before we left Sydney, I found myself scouring the Philippines Backpacker Facebook group for suggestions on what to do in the land of the 7000 islands. I befriended Matt, a CouchSurfing veteran actively engaged in the Facebook group. Matt regularly shared knowledge about his home country with curious travellers like us, who were eager to visit.

"We have no itinerary," I told him, "But we've heard it's the time of year when whale sharks are prevalent in the waters of the Philippines."

The conservationist in me ended the sentence with: "But is there an ethical way to see these creatures?"

Our common values became apparent as he shared with me that he was a volunteer for the World Wildlife Fund's (WWF) Philippines chapter. He was actively involved in a community-based whale shark ecotourism program in his hometown of Donsol.

The seaside village of Donsol, Sorsogon, is located in the western part of the Philippines' Luzon Island. Prior to 1998, the village residents survived solely off fishing the surrounding seas. The area was known for illegal dynamite fishing, one of the most destructive recreational methods of fishing. The practice involves the use of explosives to stun or kill schools of fish for easy collection. It is an uninformed practice, often undertaken by fishermen eager to sell as much catch as they can to sustain their livelihoods.

In 1998, word got out about a large concentration of whale sharks in the seas off the coast of Donsol. WWF saw the threat to the whale shark populations and so the organisation committed to helping set up a community-based whale shark ecotourism program. They educated and trained the local people and, with the support of the United Nations Development Programme, the Butanding Ecotourism Development Project was born. This project provided an alternative way of life for the people in Donsol. It brought jobs, income and infrastructure to the town and aided in the cessation of dynamite fishing.

Conor and I arrived at the Butanding Ecotourism Centre early on a Wednesday morning, directly from our rather bumpy overnight bus journey from the capital of Manila. Before we embarked on our boat tour, which Matt so kindly helped us to organise, we were invited to watch a demonstration video that outlined the rules for interacting with the whale sharks. The centre implemented rules as a way to protect the animals from harm. They had a one-boat, six-people-per-whale-shark policy and enforced a strict 4-metre distance between swimmers and the whale sharks. They also prevented any scuba diving, fishing or underwater flash photography in the area. Each boat tour provided income for one spotter, one boat driver and one Butanding interaction officer who guided guests through the experience and ensured the rules were obeyed.

After our induction we boarded the boat which departed into the vast blue ocean off Luzon's coast. It was a clear day with not a cloud in the sky as we ventured out to see the gentle giants who roam those plankton-rich waters. I was fascinated to learn how whale sharks (a creature that can grow up to eleven metres in length) survive on a diet of plankton (a creature that is often less than one inch in length).

Our skilful spotter, who stood on the bow, sighted a whale shark up ahead. The boat stopped at a safe distance.

"Get ready," our guide prompted us.

We sat on the side of the boat, snorkels set up around our foreheads, ready for our signal to jump into the water below. I looked at Conor next to me, our flippers hanging off the hull. In that brief moment, we gave each other a look that would have translated to 'I can't believe we're doing this,' as we waited for the signal.

"Now," shouted the spotter.

I fell into the sea below, trusting she would hold me. Initially, all I could see through my mask was a cloudy ocean, a sign of an abundance of plankton. Powered by adrenaline, I swam to the surface and spouted the excess water from my snorkel. I looked around beneath me. Within what felt like seconds, a grey silhouette patterned with undulating white dots came into my vision. A 6-metre-long whale shark swam graciously beneath me, its strong fins pushing it through the water at a fast pace, remoras in tow, nibbling the parasites off its spotted skin. I swam hastily to keep up, kicking my fins, but in less than a minute, the creature disappeared into the blanket of plankton beneath us.

Every second I watched that whale shark, I was mesmerised. I felt an intense connection to the world below, to the big blue. I was in her home now. But as powerful as the experience was, as memorable as that moment will always be, a part of me felt uninvited. We had taken so much, us humans. We'd marked our flags atop the highest mountains and claimed we'd conquered them. We'd stripped indigenous lands of their forests of trees and laid claim to their wood as if we had the right to destroy a living organism, send it to a woodchip mill and then sell it off to the highest bidder. And now we threatened the oceans too: with our commercial fishing vessels, our dumping ground for tonnes of plastic waste, our inquisitive playground. I couldn't help but feel it was best to leave those giants be.

I know my being in Donsol and engaging in that encounter with the whale sharks for my own curiosity was merely a dent in the capitalistic engine I existed in, but I still felt morally accountable for my actions. On one hand, the experience we had was helping to improve the livelihoods of the local population. Yet, on the other hand, were we exploiting a fragile ecosystem disguised in the name of a tourism experience? I pondered about the balance. I dreamed about a world where humans existed in harmony with nature and not to its detriment. *Could such a utopia ever exist? Was there really such a thing as an ethical interaction with whale sharks?* I couldn't be sure.

Blue was a colour so prevalent that month in the Philippines as we island-hopped to explore more of the food and culture and biodiversity the country had to offer. One month was barely enough time to scratch the surface of that incredible destination, but we did our best with the time we had.

In late May, we spent a few days in a homestay on the island of Balicasag, in the home of Rita, a member of a community homestay exchange program. Balicasag is a small island located in the Bohol Sea, roughly 8.5 kilometres southwest of Panglao. The dinky island is less than one kilometre in diameter and is home to a small community of fishermen and their families. The surrounding reefs have been declared a marine sanctuary since 1985.

Rita had opened up one of the three bedrooms in her family home to receive guests from all over the world. The home was a one-storey building constructed using concrete slabs with a generous amount of space surrounding the property, scattered with banana trees and clotheslines. The home had a large kitchen space with wooden, glass-paned cabinets full of Tupperware and cooking utensils. The bench space often accommodated bunches of ripe bananas picked from the trees outside, imported packets of tea and coffee, some drinking water and the ingredients for what was on the menu that day, which was more than likely fish caught straight from the *bangkas* (boats) off those shores.

Upon arrival, we met Rita's grandchildren and daughter-in-law, Joanne, who took the time to sit with us and explain the circumstances of life on a relatively isolated tropical island that only received six hours of electricity per day.

"We planted sweet potato, and it came out salty potato," said Joanne, referring to the quality of soil on the island. "Most of what we have here comes from Panglao, including water," she continued.

In the dry months, Rita's family head to Panglao at least once every two days to get their water supply.

"We bathe every second day just to make sure there is enough water for everyone," she explained.

I relished Joanne's storytelling. Being able to witness the vast ways of life that exist on this planet was like having my own personal David Attenborough docuseries, but it was real life. It helped me to understand more, to be grateful for more. I stopped taking for granted little things like long, hot showers and avid water pressure, or sweet potato fries stacked neatly inside a ceramic bowl, accompanied by a reasonable serving of sweet chilli sauce. I still wondered, why did we exist across such an infinite spectrum of life circumstances? Why was war raging on in one corner of Earth while the sounds of children's joyful laughter echoed in another? Our lived experiences were so contrasting, but I suppose there was also a beauty in that.

After spending the day with Rita's family and learning from them, we headed out to cool off in the animated underwater world that housed the entire cast of *Finding Nemo* and more. Vibrant coral, bright-blue starfish and the occasional giant sea urchin caught our eyes as we snorkelled in the shallows by the sands. The afternoon brought the harshest heat and so the children of nearby homes joined us by the shore. They played and frolicked until the sun faded and the temperature lowered.

As six pm came about and the electricity made its first appearance for the day, the television came on and Rita's grandchildren got to spend some time watching Cartoon Network on an old cathode-ray tube (CRT) television – a daily reward. From six pm to midnight the island centre lit up and some residents headed to the local karaoke house. If we'd learned one thing about the Filipinos, it was that they love their karaoke.

Five-peso coins hounded the jukebox as we took turns choosing our favourite tunes; the children even sang along to their own beloved Filipino pop songs. At one stage we were all dancing around a snooker table to Lionel Richie's 'All Night Long'. I bet he'd be proud to know his fans exist as far away as the Philippines, on an isolated island in the Bohol Sea, I thought.

Meanwhile, I had been given a journalism assignment by the World Fair Trade Organisation's (WFTO) Asia chapter to write about some of the fair trade initiatives happening in the Philippines. This was a dream opportunity for me – writing for a movement I cared so deeply to advocate for. I had never studied journalism but was starting to gain recognition for my storytelling abilities, specifically on the topics of social and environmental activism.

I asked Conor if he'd be interested to be my photographer and videographer for the project. After all, he hadn't much to do aside from lap up the art of presence – *il dolce far niente* (pleasant relaxation in carefree idleness). He had, however, started to work on a few of his own ideas, utilising the creative soil unearthed in the garden of his own mind as each day brought upon the evaporation of Sydney's demands.

We were to visit two projects on and off the coast of the island of Cebu, located in the Central Visayas region. One assignment was to learn and report on the plight of farmers in Toledo, specifically their fight to protect their rich, organic lands from foreign investment. The other assignment was on the island of Kinatarcan, where on 8 November 2013 category 5 typhoon Yolanda decimated the Eastern Visayas region of the Philippines, reducing buildings on islands like Kinatarcan to rubble. Both communities had built relationships with WFTO's Philippines partner, Southern Partners and Fair Trade Centre (SPFTC). The organisation was working on the ground to assist in the set-up of sustainable businesses and procure fair trade products from the communities encourage economic opportunity.

With amateur camera equipment in our backpacks and passion in our hearts, we set off from SPFTC's main headquarters in Cebu City for a few days on the road. A white *bangka*, one of many outriggers sprawled across the shallow turquoise sea, awaited us at the harbour to take us over the waters to Kinatarcan. Kinatarcan was a small island located off the northern coast of Cebu, and part of the municipality of Santa Fe. The community on the island made their daily living by fishing the surrounding seas and engaging in sustainable farming. In November 2013, all that changed.

"We thought it was the end of the world. The cyclone destroyed all our fishing boats and all our nets. We had nothing left," said local resident Margarita.

SPFTC visited the area soon after the typhoon's devastation and began to work with community members to rebuild their livelihoods. The location and climate of Kinatarcan was an optimal area to grow the enduring, nutrient-rich plant, moringa – a plant that could withstand direct heat with minimal water. It was also dubbed a super-food by mainstream nutritionists, becoming increasingly popular in the international consumer market.

"Moringa is very easy to grow and with many households on the island already growing moringa plants in their gardens, we saw this as an opportunity to create an alternative livelihood for the community, aside from fishing," said SPFTC's production officer, Nadette.

"Prior to Yolanda, unemployment was high among women in this community," Nadette said. "However, it's wonderful to see how moringa production has offered a sense of empowerment and independence for women here, especially after such difficult times."

As I interviewed Nadette and Margarita, Conor filmed and photographed some of the local women as they handled the branches of fresh moringa and prepared them for production. The Filipino women were dressed in food-safety attire with blue hair nets covering their hair, white aprons and gloves, and face masks. We were shown how the bright green, feathery herbal plant was grown, washed, dried and then run through machines to be either transformed into flakes or powder, and packed to be sold locally, or shipped to international markets. I continued taking my notes, feeling like foreign correspondent, Christina Lamb, but in a much less perilous environment.

Conor and I took a break from our reporting and sat on a nearby table beneath the shade of a makeshift tarpaulin, held up by solid sticks of bamboo. I could see patches of a cyan ocean in the distance. Perfectly shaped palm trees scattered sparsely atop the beige sand, making the scene look like a picture on a holiday postcard. I looked over at Conor. His hair had grown. It once again curled and shaded the top of his forehead. He looked like the boy I met at the Hive Bar, although with a hint of explorer. Perhaps I'd rubbed off on him.

"I'm glad you're here," I said. "It means so much to me."

Chapter 15 - Golden eras

Myanmar, formerly known as Burma, was our next destination. We were lucky enough to have found the perfect window of opportunity to visit this fragile country. 2016 was one of the few and far between peaceful periods in Myanmar's modern history, which suffered from perpetual intervals of political unrest. Htin Kyaw had been sworn in as president, ushering in a new era for Myanmar as Aung San Suu Kyi's democracy movement took power, receding fifty years of military domination.

Despite being a nation that had endured more turbulence in recent years than any other country in the Southeast Asian peninsula, Myanmar opened its borders to tourists in 1992. And while the capital of Yangon was no Bangkok or Ho Chi Minh City, it was still a bustling metropolis that exhibited cosmopolitan remnants that once allured George Orwell and inspired his first novel, *Burmese Days*.

Yangon had charisma. It was a city spread across centuries. The sight of a watchmaker, who sat slouched over his workbench on the footpath, delicately examining the pieces of a hand watch with a magnifying glass, unvexed as locals hurtled past him, reminded me of a 1920s movie. Cars parked parallel in narrow streets beneath five-storey terraces, precariously jumbled electrical wires hanging from their windows, brought me back to 2016. A young woman sitting atop a bamboo-structured market stall, gathering pieces of okra and bunching them into sets of six, her face painted with smears of thanaka, took me to a bygone decade. Wherever I looked, life was seething.

We joined a Yangon walking tour to learn more about the history of the city that was once supposedly the third-largest cosmopolitan in Asia. This was during the rule of the British who colonised Burma from 1824 to 1948. Yangon was yet another opportunistic invasion for the Brits, who had an infamous history of occupying nations in the name of economic power and imperialism.

Geo-politics often reminded me of the schoolyard, and in the late 20th-century, Britain was the bully. They scouted the grounds for whoever had the most amount of precious candy, proceeded to manipulate whoever that was, perhaps pay a few bribes here and there so the other kids wouldn't tell, and then take all the candy they darn well pleased. Once they had taken all the candy they wanted, they left behind a deficient, disheartened and dispossessed husk of a child, or in this case, a nation.

"And here we have the former Government Telegraph Office built between 1913 and 1917," our guide said as he pointed to the huge structure on Pansodan Street.

"In 1939, there were 656 telegraph offices connected by more than 30,000 miles of wire," he continued.

The building was distinctly colonial. Eighteen tall, white column pillars stood at the entrance to the six-storey edifice. It was difficult not to look at that mammoth structure and feel as if it looked down on the people of Yangon, just like the British colonists looked down on them during the late 19th-century invasion. Although George Orwell's, *Burmese Days,* was fictional, the proclaimed author disguised his anti-totalitarian political views into the words of that story, subtly portraying the ways in which the colonists disregarded and exploited vulnerable people.

In the novel, the character of John Flory was cast as a liberal, albeit hedonistic, English trader who worked as a manager for a timber firm. I admired the way Orwell weaved Flory's centrist political views about colonialism into the story. In some ways, I felt Flory could be a man who existed today, with the same trials and tribulations as a man back in the Burmese days of the 1920s.

'Of course, I don't deny,' Flory said, 'that we modernise this country in certain ways. We can't help doing so. In fact, before we've finished, we'll have wrecked the whole Burmese national culture. But we're not civilising them, we're only rubbing our dirt on to them. Where's it going to lead, this uprush of modern progress, as you call it? Just to our own dear old swinery of gramophones and billycock hats. Sometimes I think that in two hundred years all this—' he waved a foot towards the horizon— 'all this will be gone—forests, villages, monasteries, pagodas all vanished. And instead, pink villas fifty yards apart; all over those hills, as far as you can see, villa after villa, with all the gramophones playing the same tune.'

Progress – it's such a subjective word, isn't it? What does it mean to *progress*? Who decides when we have advanced as a society? And what does advancement mean? Are pink villas fifty yards apart a sign of an advanced society? Are glass-paned skyscrapers, towering over cemented footpaths and tarmacked roads for vehicles emitting more carbon than the few scattered sidewalk trees could ever possibly absorb, a sign of an 'advanced' society? Or is progress an antilogy – an idea that is solely influenced by the observer? The more I thought about it, the more it seemed like progress was as much a lenticular illusion as the blue or gold viral dress phenomenon of 2015.

We continued our walking tour, weaving through the street vendors on Anawrahta Road. The smell of fried spices wafted in our direction. Conor and I followed the scent and decided to take a pit stop at one of the makeshift food stalls. Small red, plastic stools, not much taller than a foot high, lined the surrounds of a wooden counter. A young Burmese man in a blue and white pinstriped buttoned-up shirt stood behind it. Next to him was a large silver pot, five jars of spices and three packs of vermicelli noodles, protected beneath a pink net that seemed to be erected to keep the flies away.

"*Mingalaba*," said the young man, greeting us with a slight bow.

Conor and I squatted down on the red stools in front of the counter. The last time I'd sat on chairs that small was in kindergarten. They were certainly too small for Conor, but he managed to keep his intact without snapping the legs and embarrassingly falling to the pavement.

We ordered a serving of *mohinga* (noodles) and watched the young man prepare them, mixing together a concoction of spices like turmeric, lemongrass and chilli. As the man handed me a plate, I thanked him, before turning to the camera Conor was holding which was recording the experience. I felt like Anthony Bourdain in *Parts Unknown*, speaking to the camera about the flavours I was tasting and about the cooking methods I had witnessed. In the background, the streets were teeming with locals while we sat there, immersed in the heart of Yangon. I was deep in culinary curiosity until the moment we both realised the microphone wasn't connected to the camera and so there was no sound to our footage. We laughed at our amateurish attempts as aspiring travel vloggers. I think that was the moment I decided I'd stick to writing.

The streets of downtown Yangon were easily navigated by a grid structure of parallel, numbered streets, similar to that of New York City. I caught myself gawking at locals, their distinctly painted faces an uncommon sight for a girl like me. Their faces were smeared with thanaka: the Burmese version of sunscreen, yet much less discreet. It was a paste made using a mixture of water and the bark of a thanaka tree and left a yellowish-white mask over the skin on which it was applied. The Burmese people would usually apply the mask to the cheeks and forehead to protect their skin from the sun. It became a distinguishing visual characteristic for the nation's people.

I quickly fell in love with that distinguished place and its unrivalled peculiarities. Conor and I spent three weeks travelling the country overland. We spent some days in the Bagan archaeological zone, marvelling at the thousands of pagodas that scattered like tilted red-clay-brick chess pawns. We cycled through the Burmese countryside of Mandalay, caught a glimpse at the world's largest book, located in the Kuthodaw Pagoda, and took a historic train ride from Kalaw to Inle Lake, on century-old rail tracks through iridescent olive hills.

There, we spent a day with a local fisherman on an Irrawaddy boat and learned about the distinctive phenomenon of cooperative fishing: a practice whereby local fishermen and Irrawaddy dolphins collaboratively fish together. The dolphins observe the calls of the fishermen and round up schools of fish into their nets. This phenomenon began many years ago but slowly faded over time. Sadly, along with the population of Irrawaddy dolphins.

"When I first became a fisherman there were many dolphins in our region. The dolphins would learn to hear our calls and come to us in packs. They would work with us to fish. We would get our share and they would get theirs. We still work with them today but there aren't many dolphins left," explained Mingun village leader, Moung Li, who had been fishing with Irrawaddy dolphins since 1984.

Although parts of Myanmar seemed frozen in time, an unrelenting new era augmented around people like Moung Li. Perhaps he wouldn't live to see whether or not the populations of Irrawaddy dolphins continue to decline or if a time would come when they thrive again, like in the years of the mid-late eighties. At least he would always know his golden era. We all deserve our golden eras, no matter how fleeting they may be.

From golden eras to golden stupas, Conor and I continued our journey through historic Burma. We travelled through the central region of the Shan State to see the Kakku pagodas and then down to the low-lying lakes and monolithic limestone mountains of Hpa An, in the southern Kayin State. It was there we would cross overland at the Mae Sot Thai border to continue on to our next destination: Vietnam.

Vietnam cradles the eastern mainland of Southeast Asia. The roughly 300,000 km² land mass stretches from China's most southern border to Cambodia's most southern border, exhibiting an immense amount of diverse topography. Thrill-seekers usually choose to navigate Vietnam in one of two directions, north to south or south to north: Ho Chi Minh City to Hanoi or Hanoi to Ho Chi Minh City. We didn't flip a coin on the decision, but both agreed we would start in Hanoi and travel south.

I admired how every country in Asia embodied its own distinct culture. Specifically, idiosyncratic attributes that made one feel as though they knew exactly where they were on this vast planet. In my mind, for Vietnam, it was the *nón lá* (leaf hat), a triangular bonnet that formed a perfect point at the apex and somewhat resembled a bamboo lampshade.

On the day we first arrived in Hanoi, as I strolled along the sidewalks of the Old Quarter, narrowly avoiding collisions with motorcycles as they bolted past me with such distanced precision that I felt the wind in their haste, I was reminded of my returned presence in that spectacular country. Two women stood beside their bicycles by the sidewalk, nón lá's atop their heads and baskets attached to the rear dropout of their bike frames. The baskets bore contents of ripe pineapples, lychees, bitter melon, morning glory and Ceylon spinach. I watched one of the women as she appeared to be haggling with a customer on the cost of the vegetables for the day. I was mesmerised for a moment, oblivious to the chaos of Hanoi that surrounded me.

"Let's find some *bánh mì*," Conor said, attracting my attention.

Bánh mì is a traditional Vietnamese sandwich filled with ingredients such as cucumber, carrots, coriander, soy sauce, chilli paste, and a pâté generally made from pork, duck or chicken liver. The ingredients are served in a baguette, the French influence that made bánh mì the fusion of two starkly contrasting cultures. The French colonisation, or rather invasion, of Vietnam, lasted over six decades from 1877 to 1954, influencing not only cuisine but language, architecture and culture as well. Vietnam regained its independence in 1945, but the people kept the prized baguette and transformed it into what is now one of the most widely recognised Vietnamese foods around the world.

We found a local nook serving the delicacy and proceeded to order, along with a Hanoi beer to chase down our food.

"No coriander please," I asked politely, interrupting the Vietnamese woman behind the counter as she reached for the bowl of green herbs. She looked at me with a mildly confused grin.

"Coriander for me though, please," said Conor, ensuring my fussy eating habits wouldn't deter him from experiencing a bánh mì with the lot.

I was, unfortunately, an avid coriander hater. Some would even say I had the 'cilantro gene', a scientifically validated phenomenon whereby certain individuals exhibit a variation in a group of olfactory-receptor genes. This unlikely variation means that, to those people, coriander tastes like soap. Not that one would necessarily know what soap tastes like unless one was a potty mouth whose parents or guardians adopted a rather nasty form of punishment. Nonetheless, I was going to have to navigate a gauntlet of the soapy-tasting herb as I spent the next month in a country that garnished itself with it.

We sat down on the small, seated tables out the front of the venue. The crumbs of the freshly baked baguette fell beneath us like snowflakes. How was the bread always so fresh? I thought to myself as I watched Conor devour his bánh mì, coriander and all. Motorcycles sped past us, but we were unfazed by the noise now. We were a part of it, an obbligato in the song of Hanoi.

"It looks like there are regular buses to Sapa. It's a six-hour journey," I said to Conor as I scoured Google for information about our next destination.

I was appreciative of our organic, collective spontaneity. We seldom had a grand plan or a jam-packed itinerary. We flowed, just like the wind. I enjoyed travelling like that and so far, that year, the wind seemed to guide us without much of a storm. Except for that one time. We hadn't realised to enter the Philippines we would need to prove a return flight out of the country. We looked at each other in disarray at the airport check-in counter and proceeded to pick a departure date like we were playing a game of roulette.

"Flight on May 15?" I said.

"Sounds good enough," Conor responded, wiping the bead of sweat from his forehead, an indication of the minor kerfuffle.

We are a species that tends to make a lot of plans, aren't we? Plan for your travels. Plan for your finances. Plan for the day ahead. Plan for a thousand days from now. Plan for the day you retire. There is a seemingly incessant need to control so many aspects of our lives. And we grasp them so tightly without remembering that those moments, that future we plan for, is not promised to us.

I often pondered about what it meant to truly surrender and let go of that need to control – to be like the flowers and almost every other being in the natural world and simply trust that all will be as it is intended to be. There is a fine balancing act between "save enough money for your retirement" and "live every day like tomorrow will never come." Perhaps the answer lies in a bit of column A and a bit of column B, or all of column B, but that isn't always possible as products of regimental societies that inject fear into our veins.

Like Thailand, Vietnam is well connected by efficient and rather comfortable buses, so we booked a last-minute bus journey to Sapa, in the country's northwest. Sapa is situated in the mountainous province of Lào Cai. Verdant hills are scattered across the horizon beneath low-lying clouds that water the rich agricultural fields of one of Vietnam's greenest landscapes.

A host of ethnic Vietnamese minorities live in the region, with the Hmong and Dao ethnicities the most prominent. Since the post-war era of the 1980s, the town centre has thrived on tourism and communities have become largely influenced by foreign visitors. Over the years, many of the ethnic tribes sort new income from these visitors and it has become a common sight to see local women, dressed in their traditional hand-embroidered garments, selling souvenirs as daily busloads of tourists flock to the region.

The bus pulled into the main Sapa bus station in the early afternoon. Outside the bus window, I could see groups of traditionally dressed Hmong women in navy blue tunics with conspicuous stripes of red, yellow and green on the sleeves and skirts, and matching knee-high socks. They each carried bags of what appeared to be shawls and scarves for sale.

Before the bus had come to a halt, at least twenty women approached us, their voices shouting over one another.

"Where are you from?" "Do you have a hotel?" "We have the best price."

It was overwhelming at first. The mayhem stole my focus from the spectacular hilled ranges surrounding us. Conor and I maneuvered our way through the crowd and into a clearing. I took a deep breath. Those were the sights of tourism I disliked the most. They seemed to strip away any authenticity from the cross-cultural interaction while simultaneously promoting a sense of exploitation.

I understood why it was that way. Many of the region's ethnic minorities are disadvantaged and the quality of life is much poorer than in Vietnam's cities. Many rely on agriculture as a means of income, which is a high-risk, low-reward occupation at the mercy of uncontrollable weather influences. And so, tourism has become a beacon, an opportune pathway to economic respite. However, when communities become dependent on tourism in that way – when tourists are seen as saviours – it preserves a colonialist history of hierarchy, supremacy and oppression.

Renowned travel writer and solutions storyteller, JoAnna Haugen, has spoken a lot about this in her work as she debunks the myth that tourism should be traveller-focused:

... instead of letting destinations flourish on their own, tourism often shapes people and places, forcing them to remould themselves into what is most desirable for travellers and the tourism industry. Over time, this has turned many destinations into places where tourism determines value versus places where tourism adds value.

What we witnessed in Sapa was a prime example of this – without regulation and awareness, I wasn't too sure how the region would fare. Nevertheless, we continued to walk forward with integrity and embraced our connection to the community there.

The crowds had dwindled and Conor and I found ourselves in conversation with a woman named Vu. Her energy was gentle, and I felt trust form between us. She explained to us that she and her sister ran their own homestay cooperative in the hills and invited us to stay overnight with them. So, as the intrepid travellers we were, we kindly accepted their offer. At least we cut out the middle-man, I thought to myself after hearing about the self-serving travel companies who acted as agents for the women in Sapa, stealing up to eighty percent of the profits made by the sale of an overnight stay in a Hmong home. *Always someone trying to get ahead.*

The next morning, Vu and her sister, Shosho, met us at our guesthouse. We strolled through the town centre and towards the verdant hills, our bright-coloured purple ponchos sheltering us from the rain that had decided to accompany us that day.

Vu led the way, the pink and green patterned scarf flawlessly wrapped atop her head ensuring we wouldn't lose sight of her. The further into the hills we walked, past the stray herds of goats, past the hemp plantations and closer towards the clouds, the further away the town centre appeared, until it was a mere Lego village engulfed by trees. Asian buffalo toddled along the sides of the dirt roads. Traditionally dressed women carried vegetables in hand-woven bamboo baskets on their backs. We watched the farmers working in the rice fields, cultivating the land with scythes and sickles in their hands. Once again, I was transported in time. I had taken a DeLorean adventure to an era long before industrialisation. It was peaceful there, perceptibly harder though.

Vu's standalone wooden home sat among a bamboo forest, on a ledge that overlooked rice fields. She lived there with her husband and three children and allowed guests to sleep on the second level of the home, on a bare mattress beneath a pink mosquito net that hung from a pillar above. The simplicity of the amenities had stopped fazing me long before we got to Vietnam. I'd slept in homes made of wood, dried cow dung, bamboo and clay. I'd slept in hammocks in the jungles of the Cardamom Mountains in Cambodia. I'd spent a night sleeping on a feeble, straw mat beneath a tarpaulin somewhere deep in the heart of the Gunung Leuser National Park in Sumatra, Indonesia. There was a sturdy resiliency that built up when one spent time experiencing the variety of ways to inhabit a home. And when one had been trekking uphill for half a day, any kind of flat surface would make for a reasonable bed.

I'd learned in my life that what really made a home comfortable wasn't the bed you lay on, but the way you felt inside those walls; the love and kindness you received, the conversations you had and the memories you made there. Home really is where the heart is, and I felt more conviction in that statement as my journey progressed.

That evening, Vu invited us to assist with dinner preparations. We sat around the fire pit of her home, learning to make traditional spring rolls by carefully placing ingredients such as carrots, cabbage and rice noodles into the rice paper, wrapping the paper like a Christmas present and then leaving the spring rolls to be fried in a pan over the fire. With a few fresh ingredients grown in the fields surrounding her home, Vu put together a Vietnamese feast that nourished the seven of us.

The ethnic Vietnamese communities in Sapa lived incredibly self-sustainably and were deeply connected to their land. I felt I could learn a lot from them. Not the least of which would be how to tend to a vegetable patch, so it produces sufficient yields. Perhaps they should have substituted my school lessons on algebra for some lessons in agriculture. I don't recall ever needing to rely on Pythagoras theorem to get me from one day to the next.

Later that evening, after the children went to bed, Vu's husband brought out a bottle of rice wine for the occasion and taught us the equivalent of "cheers" in Vietnamese.

"Mot, Hai, Baa, Zoorr!" he shouted as we sipped the potent liquor.

As the evening went on, we conversed with Vu and her husband as best we could. We'd been gifted another opportunity to feel deeply connected to the places we visited and the people who offered us a home.

Just as we had intended, Conor and I ventured south. We biked the magnificent Hai Van Pass from the iconic beaches of Da Nang to the imperial city of Hue, and then decided to spend my thirtieth birthday in one of the prettiest towns in Vietnam, Hội An.

Thirty was such a milestone. I was elated about it but also intimidated by the new era that lay ahead. I was bidding farewell to an entire decade, one-third of my existence. I could no longer call myself a twenty-something-year-old. I was thirty-something now. On a positive note, birthdays signified growth, and I had grown a lot in those years. I had changed in more ways than I could have ever fathomed.

When I was sixteen, I imagined what life would be like at twenty-two. I imagined I'd be married and beginning to start a family. After all, that was the age my mother had me. Twenty-two seemed a long enough way away to assume that I'd be adulting in some form, that I'd be living out my grand life plan.

Then, when twenty-two approached and I was adulting in a much less responsible and less sober way – and grand life plans were thrown out the window – I figured twenty-six might be the year I "settled down" or "had it all together." And then, twenty-six approached and I was gladly not the person I thought I would become. I was a fraction of that naive sixteen-year-old who once existed sometime in the new millennium.

Ageing is an exciting process once you gather enough years to reflect back on who you once were. However, it seems no matter how much you imagine or perceive yourself in the future, you may never fully know who you might be until that day arrives. At twenty-six, a person told me I would change so much from twenty-five to thirty. I didn't believe them until thirty greeted me and I was a fraction of the naive twenty-six-year-old who once existed sometime in the new millennium.

To this day, Hội An is one of the prettiest provinces I have ever visited. The charming, riverside, World Heritage-listed town exhibits Chinese and Japanese influence from the 15th and 16th centuries when it acted as a trading port. Coloured paper lanterns decorate the bicycle-friendly streets, a traditional Japanese wooden bridge connects one side of the inlet to the other. The buildings are painted in bright colours – canary yellow with dark green doors, baby blue with crimson red doors. To wander through those streets was like living in your very own Vietnamese fairytale. And I felt like a princess. For a fleeting moment, I was up in my fairytale castle. But that was soon about to change. I'd forgotten that, like the pappus of the dandelion, our fairytales are also fleeting.

As Conor and I ventured closer to our final destination in Vietnam, a subtle distance began forming between us. Almost three months had passed since he left Sydney to accompany me on my journey. In the previous weeks, I had started to witness signs from him of a longing for stability. That, perhaps, the novelty of life as a vagabond was wearing him thin. At the very least, the financial stresses had reared their head. I'd picked up some of the financial responsibility in Vietnam because, on a subconscious level, I wanted our journey to stay on for as long as possible. And maybe, in an unconscious act of selfishness, I didn't want him to leave. I didn't want to be alone.

The instinctual knowing that a time would soon come for Conor to leave and go back to Sydney evoked a familiar feeling. I thought about Dean, about that time almost one year prior when he told me he couldn't accompany me on the journey. It was a déjà vu moment, but a multiverse version: a few set changes, a different pair of shoes, a different country. I knew I hadn't healed from that, but I masked it well. I thought about what my mother said to me as she witnessed the aftermath of my previous heartbreak: 'I think you need this time on your own, to know yourself.'

I'd often struggled with detachment. Perhaps it was a childhood trauma response from dealing with the separation of my parents at such a young age. Our learned behaviours in the earliest years of our lives can emerge much later in life. It is a hardwire embedded so deep within our psyche that it can take an immense amount of metacognition to untangle. I hadn't gone there yet. I was wounded by the thought of being alone. Maybe I did need this time on my own, but I was conflicted.

When it comes to the transformational journey one takes after an end to a relationship: the solo quest to "find oneself," there is an inherent contradiction. Because, yes, in some ways solitude is a friend of healing, but community, togetherness and connection are also confidants. It is often through our relationships with others that a mirror forms and we are able to see our reflection in them. We are able to feel the dynamics in which we show up around them, and observe the innate workings of our interpersonal relations, uncovering parts of ourselves that are hidden beneath the complex layers of our human existence.

I believe no person comes into our life without an inevitable purpose. It is only when looking back on when, why and how this other soul crossed our path that we can see the way in which they watered our garden in order for us to flourish, or wither. Let's not forget, withering is a form of flourishment in itself because, in order for the flowers to bloom in spring, the leaves must wither in winter.

One sunny afternoon in early July, Conor and I visited the Valley of Love Park in Da Lat, a rather peculiar theme park popular with Vietnamese newlyweds and located among beautiful gardens nearby the Hồ Đa Thiện lake.

We strolled through the gardens, admiring the odd, novelty statues and sculptures scattered throughout the park: a replica of Cinderella's pre-pumpkin carriage; a two-metre tall, hedged peacock, the walls of its tail fanned out and covered in red and pink quince blossoms; and a perfectly trimmed hedge maze with corridors leading to somewhere. As we approached the entrance to the maze, I confronted Conor on the topic which we had both been avoiding.

"I can sense that you've been thinking about home," I said to him as we navigated the corridors of the maze which ironically, when viewed from above, was in the shape of a heart.

"I know," he said. "You know I wish I could stay with you. It's just that I need to go back to work, to my life back there. You can't sustain both of us on this journey."

I watched as the roots of Sydney called him back like a Venus flytrap. Back into its safety net. Back to the incessant responsibilities, a life governed by rules, laws and expectations.

"I could," I said with disavowal.

"It wouldn't feel right," he responded.

"So does that mean you're leaving after Saigon?" I said, trying to hold back any signs of emotion.

Conor walked towards me. I looked at his sun-kissed, scruffy-bearded face. It was the face of a man who had trodden thousands of miles by my side, a man who had shown up for me, who had accompanied me on a long journey across a mighty continent when another would not. He took my hands and looked deep into my eyes, crushing the confrontation like cold water.

"You've changed my life," he said, his words showering me with bona fide love.

I knew that was the prequel for a goodbye. I searched for any anger inside of me, but there was none. In its place, there was gratitude. Gratitude for a boy who bandaged a wounded girl with the threads of his heart and took a chance on her. Perhaps our journey was only ever meant to be the time we met over margaritas at the Hive Bar and then backpacked across Southeast Asia on a shoestring. Two carefree, barefoot lovers surfing the winds.

It would take some months before my heart mended from the separation from Conor because it wasn't only one wound to mend. The threads he had used to sew my already broken heart had raptured, unveiling a wound that ran far, far deeper.

Despite the exacerbated grief and sadness I was now carrying, there was a stubborn, determined voice inside of me that insisted I keep pushing on. Sri Lanka was the next destination, followed by India and then Nepal. And so, I threw myself back into my writing and into accomplishing the dream I had to spend one year in Southeast Asia, no matter what personal challenges got in my way.

Chapter 16 - Déjà vu

As the plane touched down at Bandaranaike International Airport, I immediately sensed a change in my usual energy. Six months prior, I would have felt stomach butterflies upon landing in a new destination like Sri Lanka. I would have been skipping through the airport singing "zippedy-doo-da" all the way to the exit. I would have sat in awe, looking out the taxi window at my new surroundings, being so grateful to be there and researching all the wonderful, impactful things I could do. That's how it usually worked. That's the feeling many of us yearn for when we travel outside our borders – outside our comfort zones. Yet, that excitement was absent. I was depleted. A flat tyre, a deflated air balloon. The joy wasn't there anymore, evaporated by loss, longing, fatigue and instability.

I spent the next few days at The Vintage Club Hostel in Mount Lavinia, hiding away in my room like a turtle in its shell. I longed for a safe space, something familiar: the arms of a friend, the feeling of my feet in the golden sands of Sydney's beaches, the gentle waves of the Pacific Ocean washing up on the shore and covering my ankles, soothing me with a crisp chill.

Our personal hardships affect us in unique ways. Some of us long for solace. Some of us find incessant distractions to avoid the feelings altogether. Some of us reach for the bottle. Some of us reach for the pills. But, I wondered, if we approached our hardships differently, could they be perceived as sensory illusions influenced by the way in which we appraise them? Hardships can be observed as opportunities or lessons in this school of life. How will we ever learn if everything in life comes easy to us? There is a certain level of growth to be found during the times our souls wander in darkness, searching for light. But when our ego can't see this, when the ego clings to the hardship itself, when it clings to what we have lost; to our unmet expectations, those lessons can be hard to decipher.

At the time, my ego had a hold on me. She clung to the loss like a child who had their favourite toy ripped from their arms. I had once again lost my safety net, a person who I'd made my home when everything around me was constantly changing. Perhaps there is an inherent need in us humans for stability, some kind of constant – a centre point to know where we are. While I loved the thrill of gallivanting around the globe and witnessing the kaleidoscope of culture and nature that this world has to offer, there was something ungrounding about it. And I'd recently started to witness how I searched for that grounding in another; how 'home' became a person, and when that person was gone, the dissonance sent me spiralling into challenging emotional states.

I met some dark moments during those days in Sri Lanka, and I habitually searched externally for the light, without understanding that I was never going to find the light outside of me. It was not there. The light I was looking for was inside. But I couldn't find the way in. I had no key. So, I continued to search. Relentlessly.

The most I saw of Colombo that year were the walls of The Vintage Club Hostel and the scenery of the route that the taxi took from Mount Lavinia back to Bandaranaike International Airport. I literally checked out.

Guests of the hostel were invited to leave painted handprints on a common wall with a parting message about their time in Sri Lanka. I grabbed a paintbrush and proceeded to mix green and yellow paints together to form an earthly blend. Gently, I used my right hand to paint strokes along the palm of my left hand until my palm was covered in a moist layer of paint. I pushed my hand firmly against the wall. Beside my childlike handprint, I wrote,

Dear Sri Lanka. I'm sorry. I'll be back soon.
Love, The Altruistic Traveller.

The night before, I'd searched the internet for the most affordable flight to the closest place that would offer me any kind of respite. I was desperate to clutch onto the nearest thing that would relieve my pain. It wasn't a packet of dark chocolate Tim Tams or a lychee martini. I needed solace. And so, I booked a one-way ticket to London to fall into the arms of my old friend from high school, Stephanie, and shower myself with alleviating comforts like chocolate bars and blueberry cheesecake, Sunday roasts and pinot grigios.

Steph and I had been friends since we were eleven years old when we attended the same high school in Glebe, a suburb located in Sydney's inner-west. Although we didn't hang out in the same schoolyard group, we bonded at weekend netball games as she defended the centre of the field, and I defended the goalpost. In high school, Steph usually hung out with the sporty girls while I hung with the … well, the inbetweeners, the ones who didn't really fit any genre but connected over our singularities and created a convergence of quirky anomalies. My two best friends in high school were Danielle and Ashleigh. We also met when I was eleven as I navigated the grounds of a new school – a lone wanderer who didn't know a single soul because my family chose to place me in a high school far from where I attended elementary. I recall my last day of elementary school, crying my little heart out because I was the only one of my friends who wasn't attending a nearby school. I was devastated, feeling as though I'd walk this world alone for the rest of my days. And then I met Danni, a poised, charismatic girl from Five Dock who approached me on the morning of 10 February 1998 and asked me to be her friend. Our journey as best friends began that day – two young girls dressed in the compulsory attire of baby blue tunics and wide-brimmed beige hats with matching ribbons wrapped around them, arguably one of the most hideous private school uniforms known in existence. That wouldn't be the last of the dreadful fashion ensembles ahead of us. We lived through trends like crimped hair, cropped

142

boleros and jeans so low at the waist that if you dropped something on the ground you wouldn't dare bend over to pick it up. I loved navigating life with her though, and when Ashleigh joined us soon after, we became three. *The three.* We were inseparable, unstoppable, navigating a life of abiding, irreverent shenanigans with our hands and hearts intertwined. I don't know how I could've made it through life without those two, albeit we did get ourselves into quite the amount of self-inflicted mischief as teenagers. We made it, though. And decades on, we still celebrate our frien-iversary on the 10th of February each year.

Steph's and my friendship also grew after high school and beyond, from underage drinking parties to multi-faceted music festivals; to trips to Mexico and impromptu break-up emergencies. There was something profound about those friendships that managed to evolve with us through time. Years became like the foundations of a home. The longer the friendship, the harder it was for the home to deteriorate.

Steph had moved to London a few years prior as part of a trend of single almost-thirty-somethings from Australia who felt the isolating geographic location, and the collectively inherent keeping-up-with-the-Joneses culture, wasn't a place for a single almost-thirty-something to thrive. The word around the block was that Londoners had more fun. I suppose it would be tough not to in a city of 9 million people and over 3500 pubs.

I stayed in her Islington share-house for a few weeks while I contemplated my next move. I wasn't sure if I had the energy in me to continue on to India and then Nepal. I'd lost a lot of the motivation that fuelled me when I first left Australia. My spark was dim. I hadn't earned a decent income in months, and I was feeling as though there was no reimbursement for my work, financial or emotional. I had put so much effort into writing stories that hardly anyone read. It seemed good news didn't stand out. Cat videos got more views than good news. Memes got more views than good news. Ten of the most

Instagrammable swings in the world got more views than ten animal conservation projects to support. Bleeding hearts and planting trees weren't exactly trending on Twitter. It was apparent that either apathy loved company, or ignorance was bliss.

That year, I had been exposed to the great juxtapositions of this earth, and it wasn't always easy to witness. I'd spent time in the sprawling slums of Baseco in Manila, where families resided in homes made entirely of scrap metal, earned a living by sorting through the city's garbage at the going rate of 10 pesos (20 cents) for a kilogram of anything valuable, and ate from local food stalls serving up *pagpag*; made from the food waste discarded by Jollibee and Mc Donald's, which catered to the fast-food addictions of the city's wealthier citizens. I'd visited families who resided in shanty homes made of wooden planks and tin sheets, situated only three blocks from Siem Reap's five-star Sheraton Hotel where the cost of a room for a night would be more than anyone in that commune would earn in one year. I met families who weren't able to afford three meals a day let alone to put their children in school. I spoke with landmine amputees who'd been shunned from society for their differences and forced into a life of homelessness. And in one of the most heart-wrenching recollections, I'd witnessed a mother demand her own child approach me and ask me for money, as she watched, peeking behind the corner of a building as if I wasn't able to see her forcing her own offspring into a practice of begging.

After those experiences, I no longer lived with a veil over my eyes. I saw the world in vastness, but it was beginning to feel as though each time I witnessed injustice or inequality, I lost a bit of my tenacity, like a character from a video game who loses a point every time they are wounded. In the metaphorical video game, I wasn't sure where to find the medicine box; the elixir that gave you back the points you had lost. And especially in those months – when the weight of my own disheartenment dragged me down, when I found myself wondering if I'd made any difference in the world at all – that elixir felt even further out of reach.

144

It was the evening after the day I'd sat in the armchair of the Jolie Rouge Tattoo Parlour on Caledonian Road for over three hours, as a gorgeous Italian man inked a permanent four-inch swallow on my right ribcage. I was lying in bed with the kind of fatigue caused by a prolonged rush of cortisol but thrilled about the tattoo, nonetheless. Due to the swallow's long migration patterns, sailors would often view these songbirds as a symbol of returning home safely after a long journey. To me, the swallow represented the conjunction of the freedom to soar and the journey home.

I heard a notification bell on my mobile phone and proceeded to pick it up.

It couldn't be.

There was his name. Dean. The name that made my heart skip a beat.

Hi Bianca,

Just an FYI that your domain name is renewed and good for another 2 years.

That's all it took between Dean and me. A few words behind a screen. A stick into an eternal flame that never died out. Years ago, Dean helped me set up a website for an organisation I supported in Cambodia. The domain must have been in his name and up for renewal.

I responded to his email. I had to.

Thanks so much. I really appreciate it.

I thought you should know, Conor and I broke up. Our paths went in different directions. I hope all is well in your world.

~ B.

Dean's email had come at an interesting time. I wondered if, on some magnetic, ethereal level, he sensed what I was going through. The timing was just too serendipitous.

I anxiously awaited his response, invigorated by just a few meagre words. It would have been rather late in Sydney with the nine-hour time difference, so I put my phone away and took a nap on my left side, wrapped in the humid air of London in August.

That late evening, I received a reply.

… I'm going to be honest, when I first read your email about you and Conor breaking up, I wasn't sure what I should have been feeling – whether to be empathetic, happy, sad for you or just plain nothing. So, I thought I'd sleep on it first before writing back a response.

I think I made the right decision and dreamed of gummy bears dressed as Rambo first before replying. So, speaking from personal experience (I was smiling while writing that because of the rarity of its irony), any end to a relationship is hard because it means coming to terms with an ending to a part of your life and adjusting that special comfort safety area which seemed so reliable. And now it's not there for whatever reason. Having that 'rock' is such a powerful safety net. Having that net dismantled and packed away creates a lot of uncertainty coupled with fear…

His words were mature. I'd almost forgotten how much he had a way with the written word. We stopped writing to each other like that when our relationship became victim to the monotonous routines of life in a busy city, and our collective creativity took a back seat to continuous social responsibilities.

We continued our email thread. I confided in him about how I was feeling about the writing, about my disheartenment, and my decision to either continue on or go back to Sydney. He wrote:

The worst decision is indecision. I always believe in following your heart and especially your instincts. Our bodies are designed with these chemically cataclysmic moments of clarity where our mind and soul become singular and focused on one thing. In some parts of this crazy world, this process is called passion. When you get a chance, find a quiet place where you can reflect on the original reasons why you wanted to go over there in the first place. And be 100% honest with yourself. Then ask yourself if, after experiencing your travels and writing to date, these reasons still hold as much value to you now as they did from the start. If so, then you keep going. Don't let your passion waiver from a few hurdles. Great things are born out of persistence.

It was as if, even after all this time, he still knew me. He still had all the right words to say – those piercing words that spoke to me as if he was right there with me, holding my hand as the bridge of life I walked upon swayed side to side with the winds of a passing storm.

I reflected on his words and on my own feelings. The reality was, while maybe not a million people read my stories, someone did, and that's all that mattered. I wasn't writing for me, for acknowledgement or praise. I was writing because I intended to share people's stories. The moment I stopped dwelling on who read those stories and how many people read them, my whole relationship with The Altruistic Traveller evolved. It seemed on my quest to change the world, I was given the opportunity to change myself.

The conversations between Dean and I continued and became more frequent over the proceeding weeks. His encouraging words aided me in my decision to continue on to India. But I was still weathered. I was running on empty.

Those two weeks in Southern India in late August were a feeble attempt. I was scraping the bottom of the barrel. Every step was a last-ditch effort to prove to myself I was OK and that I could achieve what I'd set out to achieve, even though I wasn't too sure exactly what that was anymore. It had been nine months of non-stop travel, two heartbreaks, one bacteria invasion and one life-altering decision to leave the place I called home for twenty-nine years.

It was only natural that I'd eventually burn out and long for a stable ground beneath me. Just like the swallow, it was time for me to migrate. And so, as I lay in an eerie, empty eight-bedroom female dormitory in Chennai, completely alone, I did what I felt was the best decision at the time and booked a flight for the next morning. Chennai to Sydney.

Chapter 17 - Unhealed wounds

I prematurely descended into a wintry Sydney after making what felt like a defeating decision to return to a place that felt most like home. One moment I was in Southern India and the next I lay beneath the pale peach walls of my father's home in a small suburb in south-eastern Sydney. The walls hadn't changed. The concrete driveway that led to the tattered wooden electric gate with the golden number two drilled into it hadn't changed. The white matte ceramic floor tiles that led down the well-lit hallway into the living room hadn't changed. But I had.

Returning to Sydney that year was like trying to fit a round peg into a square hole. I was no longer the version of me who stepped onto that plane almost one year prior. I didn't occupy the same space I had left. Instead, I was challenged to find the shape of my more recent evolution of me and fill it up, in a city that didn't know me anymore.

As I searched for comfort, I reached out to one of the people who knew my soul through each of those evolutions, my Auntie Leanne. Auntie Leanne is one of my mother's two sisters. Although she had resided in Virginia, USA, with her husband for the latter part of my adult life, we remained close, especially as I grew from a young girl into a woman and we began to observe the similarities between us – our empathetic hearts, our liberal views, our intensely critical thought processes and our deep desire to see the world in all its wholeness. On some level, I felt we were soul sisters, connecting with each other in a way that earthly language could not explain. I felt language often limited our way to describe how we felt about one another, specifically the English language. The Japanese language compensated for that dissonance with its ability to transform emotion into earnest, poetic proverbs. What Auntie Leanne and I had was *itaidōshin* (異体同心). In English, it translates to "the harmony of mind between two persons; two persons acting in perfect accord." That was us.

I expressed to her the discomfort I had been feeling about returning to a life I wasn't too sure I would ever return to. She offered me the wisdom she often so kindly delivered through her clement words. They read:

I read somewhere that there are two places the spirit resides: the mountain top, where we are inspired, exhilarated, transformed, free and fulfilled. And down in the marketplace, where most of our human interactions and challenges are and where the gravity/weight is so strong, it can keep us down – jostling, mingling, struggling at that level; and if we live like this long enough, we are absorbed by the marketplace and its incessant worries and cares and can forget the mountain top altogether, even question its existence, let alone transformative power.

I could feel the deeply apparent difference between my energy out there, on the metaphorical mountain top, and my energy in Sydney. I thought about the heart-warming time I connected with Vu in her family home in the hills of Sapa, the time we danced and sang karaoke with the residents of Balicasag island or the way I felt when I interviewed those passionate farmers who fought to protect their organic lands from foreign occupation. I was inspired and exhilarated, transformed, free and fulfilled. And now that felt like a dream, a beautiful bygone dream.

Not many people talk about the adaptability challenges faced when returning from a life-altering experience, or an extended absence. There is a re-assimilation required. That re-assimilation, coupled with the culture shock that is present if one has spent time in a paradoxical destination, makes it a rather testing undertaking to feel comfortable in a place once familiar but no longer.

Few people treat you differently though. To most, it probably seems like time has barely passed at all since you left. We all have enough going on in our own lived experiences to examine those of others. And especially, in a demanding city like Sydney, presence is an oasis in the desert.

In my case, people might have read a few of my blogs or skimmed through my Instagram captions, but most wouldn't have had the capacity to ponder on the transformational expansion I'd experienced or the rousing escapades I'd embarked on. Nor did I expect them to. But it meant I'd often downplay the conversations I had in the marketplace I returned to.

You'd ask people how they'd been. They'd say, "Same old. Not much to report on here."

They'd ask you, "How was your holiday?" and you'd cringe a little on the inside because what you experienced could hardly be defined as a holiday. But you sensed they weren't open to a long-winded answer about how watching the soft, wrinkled hands of a Kayan woman in the Shan Hills of Myanmar, as she weaved fine, coloured pieces of thread through an antique wooden loom, made you feel deeply connected to the artisans who sew and weave the clothes we wear, and how you now you refuse to step into an H&M or a Zara and support an industry that actively exploits humans in the name of profit.

So, you'd say, "It was good," and they'd say, "Back to the real world now," and you'd smile insincerely because you knew that what you experienced was more real to you than the light of day.

There were those few people, like my friend Kate, who engaged in less surface-level dialogue and asked questions that cut to the core like, "What were some of the greatest lessons you learned out there?" or "Can you remember a conversation with someone that specifically moved you?" or "How do you feel you have changed as a person since you stepped on that plane last year?" Those were the conversations I longed for the most. They were rare though, like *edelweiss*.

The purple jacarandas bloomed early across Sydney that spring and just like their renewal, Dean and I were in the midst of our own renaissance. Our dialogue over the preceding weeks had escalated and we found ourselves quite effortlessly back at a place of deep endearment. We had arranged to meet that week opposite the Strawberry Hills Hotel on the corner of Devonshire and Elizabeth Street in Sydney's Surry Hills. The location was sentimental. It was where we had met for our first date over two years beforehand, one mid-winter evening as we shared an Italian meal over a red and white chequered tablecloth, our hearts unbeknownst to the stellar collision which awaited us.

I stood nervously on the street corner, watching out in the distance for his tall silhouette as pedestrians passed me by, the red and green walking man swapping turns every few minutes. I arrived eight minutes before our meeting time. I knew he wouldn't be late. He was very punctual. Perhaps I should have arrived late, I thought. Those eight minutes were excruciating. It was too much time to think, to over-analyse what it would feel like to look into his eyes, to feel his soul. It had been so long. So much had happened, and although our connection laid a strong foundation, there were old scars and unhealed wounds. I knew it. We both knew it. But when we finally saw each other on the corner of that street, when the energy of adoring affection radiated around us, exploding like fireworks, we forgot about the past and fell into each other's presence like the pull of gravity to the Earth.

As Dean's and my relationship blossomed once again, I found myself re-evaluating my life back in Sydney. I had commenced looking for employment, scouring the online equivalent of the jobs section of a newspaper. Had it been 1989, I'd have a marker pen and an ashtray full of cigarette butts as I stressfully circled the adverts deemed fit for my experience. The trouble was that I did not want to go back into the same career. I had a *sine qua non* to spending the next years of my life selling my soul to another corporate giant and ending up in the same pool of anxiety that became the catalyst for my former escape from Alcatraz.

That aversion left me scratching my head as to what kind of career I was fit for. I didn't desire to become a paid journalist – the industry was too competitive, it didn't pay well, and I preferred to write for love, not for money. I thought to look for jobs in the non-governmental sector, to continue my quest to make a difference in the world, but many positions required long-time experience and a university degree. (I had deferred my feeble attempt at a university degree in 2015 because I felt it more beneficial to put that money towards experiencing the world first-hand, rather than racking up a debt that would take me years to pay off.) I then thought to apply for jobs in the travel industry because I liked to travel, evidently. However, those jobs were few and far between, with the most suitable choice being an administrative assistant for a travel booking provider, starting on a junior wage.

It would seem I was back at the bottom. I was a thirty-year-old who took a sabbatical and couldn't seem to pick up where she left off. However, I was missing one incredibly paramount ingredient back then. Something I wish I could tell any of the younger versions of myself or anyone, in fact, especially that diffident girl who seemed to have forgotten how incredible she was: *You will only ever be as capable as you believe you are.*

My limiting beliefs had me convinced that I didn't have the crossover skills required to pursue a career at the same level at which I had left the last one. Those beliefs, coupled with the unsteadiness of returning from an extended absence, left me quite frankly, insecure.

"I don't think I can handle another job rejection this week," I said to Dean as he took a bite out of the vegemite sourdough toast he had ordered from the café downstairs.

"It'll be OK," he said. "It builds up the resilience, that's for sure."

We had been enjoying each other's company and getting reacquainted after our leave of absence. Like many of the other people with whom I reunited, not much had changed in Dean's life. He was still working for the same company, still living in the same apartment block, although he had moved a few storeys higher, and still frequenting the Peaberry Café most mornings for vegemite toast with butter on sourdough and a large orange juice. There was a welcomed familiarity to that routine. It tempted me to mould myself to fit into that square hole.

Our renaissance didn't come without challenges though. Some people in Dean's immediate circle held pessimistic opinions about us being back together. It seemed they had generated their own version of our narrative by reading only one page of it: the page with the tribulations. Those people never considered reading *my* pages of the story, *our* pages of the story. In those months upon returning to Sydney, I found myself back in the lion's den of passive judgement that seemed to proliferate, like a virus, in the kinds of societies where it is more common to gossip about others' lives than to simply mind one's own business, or at the very least move forward with understanding and compassion. I would often wonder how different our stories would be if we weren't influenced by the thoughts and opinions of others, but I knew we wouldn't get there as a society until we shifted our focus towards inner peace and acceptance. One who is focused on their own path need not throw judgemental stones to obstruct the paths of others or crack the windowpanes through which they see the world.

Later that day, as I indulged in some Netflix binge-watching, I received a call.

"Hello," I answered.

"Hi, is this Bianca?"

"Yes. Speaking?" I responded.

"This is Claire from Flight Centre. We're calling to let you know you've been accepted for the position. Congratulations. We'll send over some information via email."

I hung up the phone and looked over at Dean.

"That was Flight Centre. I got the job."

There wasn't a terrible amount of elation in my demeanour. While I was glad to have finally received an acceptance offer rather than a rejection or the professional equivalent of ghosting, the pay rate was a third of what I had been earning in my former position.

"They asked me to come in for an induction on Monday," I said.

That weekend, I came down with a debilitating case of influenza. I hadn't been that ill in years. It left my throat so inflamed I could barely speak. I wondered if it was a sign, an intuitive signal to change course: *Don't do it, Bianca!*

I didn't listen. I went in that Monday with dark circles under my eyes and the gruffest voice I had ever had. Needless to say, after poorly attempting to answer two customer phone calls and inform them of flight schedules available, the manager on duty sent me back home and rescheduled my start date. That was the first and last day I ever worked at Flight Centre.

That same week, I received a phone call from another employer. They informed me that while I was not accepted for the position I applied for, there was a company in the same building that was looking for an employee with the skillsets I possessed. It was a project manager's position at a boutique digital design and development agency based in Sydney's north. The manager had been intrigued by my capabilities and the management position I held during my previous career. It seemed like a fitting opportunity. The pay was fair, and the company was small enough that I wouldn't feel like a cog in a machine, plus there was no five-storey underground car park, nor a tedious commute or lengthy hierarchy of mildly priggish males.

I didn't know it at the time, but those seemingly insignificant series of events that led me to embark on that new career path significantly influenced the next era of my life. Had anything in that chain of circumstances differed – had I not returned to Sydney from India, had I not reunited with Dean, had I not caught influenza, had the former company I had applied to work for not informed me of this other position available, had I not shown up for the interview – my life may have never turned out the way it has. Never underestimate the serendipitous magic in every small moment of life. As Steve Jobs once said, "You can't connect the dots looking forward; you can only connect them looking backwards."

As the humpback whales made their yearly migration past the shores of the Eastern Seaboard and the endemic magpies built their nests high up in the gum trees shading Sydney, I began to find routine again. It didn't take long before the alarm bells were the first sounds to ring through my ears as I woke, for the jolly staff in the café beneath the office to know my soy hot chocolate order without me having to signal anything but a smile, and for the term 'TGIF' to reappear in my vocabulary as I celebrated the arrival of a forty-eight-hour interlude. I'd been absorbed by the marketplace. And after a few months, the transformational journey across borders became *that one time I went backpacking through Southeast Asia.*

While learning the ropes in my new career, I attempted to maintain a small hold on my blog and the presence I had found in the social-impact arena. I volunteered with the Fair Trade Network of New South Wales and Amnesty International, both not-for-profit organisations that aligned with my core values of equality and empowerment. I kept up to date with local advocacy events around town, attended marches for human rights and frequented informative seminars that would allow me to continue to keep conversant about pressing social and environmental issues and the solutions being crafted for them. Keeping a foothold in those communities of like-minded people felt like grasping for air as Sydney pulled me back into its rapid undercurrent. But it required a lot of cognisant effort to stay connected to community, to not get dragged beneath the rapids into a pattern of insensible escapism.

Between work, volunteering and writing, the time that seemed so abundant all those months beforehand had become scarce, like rain in the Murray–Darling Basin. On the weekends, if Dean and I weren't catching up with friends or nursing dreadful hangovers, we'd be too fatigued to engage in rousing activities like day hikes in the vast valleys of the Blue Mountains or impromptu swims in the Pacific Ocean. Days blended into weeks, weeks blended into months and one day in early January, I found myself resenting the lacklustre routine I had fallen back into.

Although I had attempted to hide the feelings of resentment from Dean, and omit them from myself, they were manifesting in other ways. He could sense my agitation. Figments of a time not too long beforehand had reared their head. We got into a big argument a few days earlier. Our unhealed wounds cried for attention. His, anger and jealousy. Mine, abandonment and irritation. We had once again met our relatively familiar crossroads – the story of a bird without roots and a tree without wings.

"Why did I even come back," I yelled, tears streaming down my face.

"I don't know what you want," Dean said, frustration in his tone. "You're unhappy here, you're unhappy there. What do you want, Bianca?"

"I ... I don't know ..." my voice trembled. I had such trouble expressing myself verbally in heightened emotional states. And that struggle only meant that the words I wanted to say but didn't know how came out in tears. I had returned to Sydney because it felt familiar, but it no longer felt like home. It was as if I was in a no-man's-land between the woman I once was and the woman I was to become. I didn't know how to become her though, and there was no going back.

When we find ourselves in that space between – in the wilderness of change – we can feel lost. It's as though the markings behind us have vanished, so we can't backtrack, and the path in front of us is not clearly marked, so we can't be certain of the way forward. I was there. I was in the wilderness, and when I searched around me, all the terrain looked the same. I didn't know which way to go, and soon a dark night blanketed the wilderness, and I could no longer see any terrain at all.

It is in those moments that surrender is our closest ally – when we are challenged to be still, to breathe and to allow ourselves to be led by our intuition, to see with our eyes closed. But I was yet to learn that. Throughout my whole life until that point, I'd been taught that we only saw with our eyes open.

Chapter 18 - A Himalayan calling

The summer of 2017 was mentally challenging. I found consolation in the repetitious routine I had established as the forty-hour work week distracted me from confronting the fact my relationship was unsteady and I had not yet planted my feet firmly on the ground. I relished the opportunities to frequent my favourite Sydney beaches such as Yarra Bay and Balmoral Beach, to bathe in the shallow, ocean shores beneath the February sun. I enjoyed being present for the adorable first-year smiles of my niece, Sienna, while sitting in the backyard of my sister's southern Sydney home and downloading the mental knots I had created in my mind with the hope the expression alone would aid in their unravelling.

"He thinks we should take a break," I said to Christina, as she nursed Sienna in her arms.

"It's tough," she replied. "You both love each other so much, but your aspirations in life are very different."

"It wasn't always this way," I said. "I feel like there is this version of us that exists outside of all of this – outside of our lives here, on some other frequency. We both feel it. But so often we can't exist there. We exist here, with the weight of expectations, schedules, normality. Sometimes, I catch that glimpse in his eye – an impelling shift in his energy. I see the person underneath all of those external influences, the person who says, 'screw it – let's fly away together, let's study philosophy, climb mountains, live in a campervan and chase sunsets.' But then the wind changes, and he is back here again. Anyway, I don't want to convince him how to live his life. If I forced him into anything, that wouldn't be unconditional love, would it?"

"Who knows, maybe you'll end up together in the end," she said.

Christina was my one biological sister and although we often didn't pass as sisters on our appearances alone, our demeanour, mannerisms, outlook on life and idiosyncratic sense of humour, accompanied by an identical, spasmodic laugh, gave it away. There was something incredibly special about sharing life with someone who saw the world through your eyes, who laughed at your silly jokes and held space for your dramatic, emotional outbursts.

"I don't know. I'm beginning to feel as though the version of love or romance that's been sold to us in the books and the movies is not about happy endings at all. Not to say it's about sad endings. The term 'ending' in itself already pulls us away from the present and into an unknown future. I just wonder how two people stay on the same path all their lives or 'till death do us part' when our own journeys of growth are so individual. I mean, in The Little Mermaid, Ariel gave up her voice to an evil sea witch just to get legs so she could be with Eric. I don't see how the idea of giving up everything for love can ultimately make someone happy forever," I rambled, down a vengeful ambush against the romanticised clichés I'd absorbed from the Disney movies in my childhood VCR collection.

"How do you make it work?" I asked.

"It's different with me and Kev," she said. "We have Sienna. We chose this life and to create a family here," she pointed around at the yard and the back patio of their one-storey brick veneer home. "And even before that, we were best friends. Like any couple, we can disagree at times. But when we do, we don't stay angry for long and end up laughing at how we can't be angry at each other. We communicate. We listen. All that stuff. We make compromises and I'm sure on some more difficult days, we both imagine what our lives would have been like had we made different choices. It's normal to think the grass is greener on the other side. Not sure if it's healthy though. Maybe in the next life, you can be the mum and I'll be the auntie that jumps on a plane on a whim," she said.

"OK, deal," I said. "But I still want to come back as a singer with a beautiful voice who can play the acoustic guitar. Just like Julia Stone."

We both laughed as a cool gust of wind soothed the air and took with it some of the unravelled mental knots of my mind.

That March, on a humid evening as a full moon illuminated the skylight above my bed, I deep-scrolled the internet and ended up on the website for Workaway, an online platform that connects travellers with short-term work opportunities in exchange for housing and cultural immersion. I was curiously combing through the search results for the keywords "volunteer" and "Nepal," just to see what might come up. It was my equivalent of window shopping. I didn't necessarily have the intent to purchase anything, but I liked how nicely the opportunities looked in the window. Although, once an attractive number caught my attention, it was hard for my mind's eye not to wonder if it might look good on me.

"Help a fair trade cooperative empowering women," read the title. The term "fair trade" intrigued me and so I clicked on the link to learn more. The organisation was located in Kathmandu, Nepal. They were looking for a volunteer to take on a three-month placement to assist with marketing, web development and overall business development. As I read through the job description, my body filled with excitement – the kind of warm, fuzzy excitement that's as if the body is signalling you. *Yes. Absolutely yes.*

Nepal was always on my radar. It contained its very own pin on my fluorescent stringed map. It came fifth on the list in the 'ten things to do in the next ten years' manifesto Dean and I had created that chianti-induced evening in the spring of 2014. And it was where I would have ended up had I not returned to Australia.

I wondered if, perhaps, I had some unfinished business with that destination: the magnificent Himalayas. Although, even if I was to entertain the idea of applying for that opportunity in Nepal and opening up the possibility of being accepted for the position, I had commitments now. I had a career, I had started to settle back into Sydney. *But were my feet planted?*

I had somehow found myself once again left with that faint, unnerving, feeling of unalignment. I thought I'd left that place. Or was it immortal? A place to revisit, on occasion, to remind us that our journeys are constantly transforming, that there is more to be learned, that there are more paths for our feet to tread. I looked seriously at the screen. I suppose it wouldn't hurt to apply, I thought to myself. I probably won't get accepted anyway, the reverse-psychology thought process continued.

The seeds we plant are so delicate: a split-second thought, a subtle mindset shift, a spontaneous click of a button on a Workaway website. I planted a seed that night, or months before, and unbeknownst to me, that seed began to grow.

The next morning, I woke to a message in my inbox. It was from Nasreen, the founder of the women's organisation in Nepal. She was impressed by my profile and wanted to set up a call with me over Zoom. Suddenly, the opportunity to travel to Nepal began to feel more real. The excitement emanated from my bones.

Nasreen's story was incredibly moving. For much of Nasreen's childhood, her world was confined by walls. In the Terai, where she was birthed on the cold earth floor of a village home, her walls were a mixture of mud and clay, a thatched roof letting in little sunlight. In Kathmandu, where she spent a portion of her childhood years as a labourer, her walls were concrete grey, with only one small, barred window admitting smog, dust and the sounds of roaring vehicles from the streets outside. Although those walls pictured different scenes, their presence represented something similar – they kept her silent.

Nasreen did not know her age. This was because in the village where she was born many women were undocumented, with no birth certificates or death certificates recorded. Women, like Nasreen, often walked their lives as the uneducated property of a patriarchal system built to exploit them as farmers, child bearers and housewives.

The villages of the Terai, situated along the southeast border of India and Nepal, represented another era. Dry plains of agricultural land enclosed small communities of huts, home to local Hindi populations. In the dry season, which occurred from March to June, the scorching heat dried the plains. Water was scarce and food even more so. During monsoon season, which occurred from July to September, it was not uncommon for torrential rains to flood the region affecting the livelihoods, food security and nutrition of hundreds of thousands of people. It was a region where poverty was rife and life was hard, especially for women like Nasreen.

"I recall my childhood coming to a halt at around age seven," she told me. "I was no longer allowed to play outside with my friends. I was told that a woman's role is to stay inside, clean the home and learn how to knead the perfect chapadi."

At the age of ten, Nasreen came to Kathmandu with the help of her brother, Majhar. "I was engrossed by thoughts of a life outside my village. I had watched the women in my village, who I looked up to, endure physical and emotional abuse. I watched my older sister forced into an arranged marriage. I witnessed the murder of my aunt and the consequent cover-up – another undocumented death of a woman. I think a deep part of me wanted to paint a different story for myself. So, one day, I followed my brother to the city."

Majhar had been taking the half-day journey to Kathmandu since he was eight years old and worked for a factory that made light bulbs. His small hands were perfect for weaving the delicate wires inside the glass panels enclosing the light. Along with many other children,

Majhar was a victim of illegal underground sweatshop labour. At the age of thirteen, he developed symptoms of asthma as a direct result of exposure to harsh chemicals like mercury vapour and argon gas. This illness prompted him to change industries and so he transferred to another trade – fashion. This was around the time that Nasreen joined her brother. The siblings were employed by an agent who sold clothing to buyers, both local and international. The way fashion supply chains operated was like a Russian babushka doll, agents inside agents. The further down the supply chain, the lesser transparency and the more human rights violations.

Their workplace was an unmarked building in Kathmandu's Dallu district, a district frequently passed by unsuspecting foreign tourists who visited the city's esteemed Swayambhunath Temple. Nasreen, her brother and four other children were placed in a room that was no larger than 10 square metres. This room was where they would eat, sleep and work.

"I recall some days I would wake up at five am and work all the way through to nine pm or midnight. We had quotas to meet and if those quotas weren't met, the agent would withhold our pay. At the end of those days, I was so exhausted I would fall asleep on the same pile of clothes my juvenile hands had been embroidering all day long," she explained to me as she described her harrowing childhood with resilience in her voice.

It was the spring of 2004 when the two-year contract for the agency came to an end. Nasreen and her brother awaited the return of their manager so they could receive their last payment and instructions on the next work placement. After several days of waiting, they realised this man had fled, along with their last two weeks of pay. Left with no other choice, the duo planned to return to their home village in the Terai. After all, Nasreen was entering her adolescence and was destined to follow the path of her predecessors into a system that would force her into marriage and inevitably silence her.

In the last week before Nasreen and Majhar intended to leave Kathmandu, Nasreen took the time to walk through the city that once overwhelmed her. She recalled the younger version of herself lifting the tattered curtain that hung over the barred windows of the factory room where she worked, ever so gently, too scared to observe the chaotic atmosphere that existed outside those walls. She was older now, and eager to stroll through the frenzied streets of Kathmandu no longer afraid. In many ways, those two years transformed her. They gave her a strength she never knew she possessed.

It was mid-afternoon and children were exiting the school grounds nearby the factory. "I remember watching the students, admiring their uniforms and their backpacks. My heart wished to have that opportunity, someone to support me and lead me in a different direction than the other women," she explained.

Nasreen's daydream was disrupted by the presence of a small brown and white dog. She jumped backwards at first, startled by the creature, but as she looked up her eyes met with the eyes of a man. He was tall, with a pale complexion, in his mid-to-late fifties. In what seemed like an instant, Nasreen's voice erupted with the words, "Teach me, please teach me?"

The man approached Nasreen gently and curiously, as the brown and white dog excitedly wagged its tail and circled around them both. They exchanged words. The man – Leslie was his name – learned about Nasreen's journey from the village to the city and the harsh working conditions that she and her brother had endured. Moved with compassion, Leslie decided to help. At first, he would bring food to Nasreen and her peers during their time of great struggle. He then offered to pay for them to rent a separate space, one where they could work ungoverned by an agent and free of exploitation. Although Nasreen's brother, Majhar, extremely protective of his little sister, felt hesitant to accept Leslie's generous offer, he knew that the option to accept support was better than returning to the village.

In the years that followed, Nasreen and Majhar made handicrafts for local businesses until a day that inspired Nasreen to broaden her mission.

"One morning, when I went to buy oranges from the local market, I noticed a woman begging in the street. I recognised her attire. The red scarf and bright yellow kurta were similar to the dress of my village. As I approached her, I noticed that she was speaking my local dialect and I was able to communicate with her. 'Why are you begging?' I asked. 'I have no money. I am pregnant and alone. I have nowhere to go,' she replied. I will never forget the look on her face. It sparked something in me. I knew I had to help her."

Nasreen explained to me how, to her, Rita represented every woman in her village she left behind. She believed that her encounter with Rita sparked what would become her underlying mission in life: to give women the voice and the equality they deserved.

Rita was one of the first employees at Local Women's Handicrafts, the name of Nasreen's entirely fair trade handicrafts business with a mission to empower and educate women, enabling them to write their own destinies. The journey to building that business into what it was back in 2017 – a social enterprise that employed over thirty-five marginalised women and inadvertently empowered thousands of women throughout Nepal – was one painted with resilience and strength.

Local Women's Handicrafts was the organisation I was to volunteer with. After connecting over that Zoom call and hearing Nasreen's story, something inside of *me* was sparked. I stood amidst the ripple effect of compassion, and I knew I would do whatever I could to support Nasreen on her mission. Call it determination, call it intuition, call it affirmation, but there are some emotional frequencies that triumph over fear and apprehension and propel us into gear like rotors on the wings of an aeroplane. There was wind beneath my wings that day, but the take-off was going to be a little turbulent.

I spent the next week over-assessing and procrastinating about how I would tell my employer that after six months at the company, I wanted to spend the next three months in Nepal. I quite enjoyed working there, so I didn't want to resign. I figured there must have been a way I could take this leave while keeping one foot in the door. But I was terrified to ask for what I wanted. Fear crept in like fog on a June morning. My mind flooded with 'what-ifs', those restricting thought patterns that keep us from stepping forward into our truth. I remembered the wise words my Uncle Luc would say to me, 'If you don't ask, they can't even say no.' His words were plausible, but difficult to implement when I wasn't used to speaking my truth. I found it so challenging to ask for what I wanted. There was a people-pleaser fragment to my personality. I didn't like to rock the boat so instead, I'd stay silent or avoid confrontation like the plague itself … unless a more powerful influence was at play, like a fierce determination to embody my innate values and continue my journey to Nepal.

It was a Thursday afternoon. I paced up and down the pavement beneath the dark grey walls of the two-storey office block located on Alexander Street. My heart was pounding. I told myself I'd break the news at 9.30 am. And then again on my lunch break. I missed those two windows of opportunity and now the day was almost over. If I didn't speak to my manager that afternoon, it would have been another excruciating day filled with anxiety. 'Just rip it off like a band-aid, Bianca,' I said to myself, desperate to emerge from the pool of stress I had self-created.

Back in the office, I swivelled my rolling chair closer to my manager's desk.

"Do you have a few minutes to chat?" I asked. "In the boardroom?"

"Sure," he answered.

We walked into the boardroom that occupied the front of the office floor. I pulled the window blinds down to shade us from the afternoon sun that met the corner block. I could sense Nigel knew it was going to be a confronting discussion. No employee asks to speak to their manager one-to-one unless they're resigning, asking for a pay rise or have a complaint to file. While my reasoning wasn't exactly a resignation, I figured I'd save the small talk, and my own sanity, and cut to the chase.

"An opportunity has come up for me to volunteer with a women's organisation in Nepal for three months and I'd like to take it," I said, palms as sweaty as an actress before the curtains opened.

"OK," Nigel replied, nonchalantly. "That does sound like an exciting opportunity and certainly up your alley."

The energy between us had calmed. The instantaneous relief I felt simply saying what was on my mind made me wonder why I didn't tell him about this sooner.

"I'd still like to work here though, perhaps drop down my hours for those three months. But I understand if that wouldn't work for the company," I said, insinuating that we had options to work with.

"Well, you're a valuable employee and we'd hate to lose you, so let's see a way we can work this out. Send me the dates you plan to be away, and we can go from there."

"OK, that sounds great. Thank you for understanding. I really appreciate it."

Nigel ran a rather progressive ship in the office. It was encouraging to work for a company that put employee well-being at the forefront of its operations and didn't succumb to the two-hundred-year-old employment structure of the industrial revolution that seemed to hang around like a bad smell. In my former career, everything was so rigid. You could hardly sneeze without having to get a doctor's certificate or some kind of proof you were one-hundred-and-ten percent unwell to sit at your office desk for the day. Working for Nigel felt like I had gone from Blockbuster to Netflix. He had successfully, albeit assiduously, created an innovative, people-centric workplace and for the first time in a long time, I felt valued.

On the way back to my desk, I took a slight detour outside for some fresh air. I was on that post-anxiety high when the glucose is still gliding through your bloodstream like wave riders at Duranbah but you're not fearful anymore, just overwhelmingly perky. I could hardly believe what had happened. I had to channel some of that energy somewhere, to spread the glorious news, so I reached for the phone in my pocket and tapped on the favourite's icon. There were three names on the list – Dean, my Uncle Luc, and my sister, Christina. I wanted to call Dean, but we had been reducing our contact since deciding to take a break from our relationship. The resistance to tapping his name was weak. Distancing myself from him was like giving up chocolate. But it was important we took the space, so I dug deep to find some restraint. It seemed some of the most profound human sufferings arose when we couldn't have the things we wanted, I thought.

I scrolled past his name, pressed 'Christina' on the touchscreen of my phone and listened to the rings.

"Hey," she answered.

"I'm going to Nepal, Chris!" my exuberant voice echoed through the phone.

"That's great news. What did your boss say?" she replied.

"He said he'd be happy to keep me on as an employee and that I might be able to work remotely a day or two while I am there."

"I'm so excited for you," she said. "It looks like the Himalayas are calling your name."

In the weeks leading up to Nepal, so many pieces came into alignment. Life felt strangely effortless, and opportunities were already beginning to present themselves to me like *hors d'oeuvres* at a dinner party. I had been contacted by a variety of organisations in Nepal who'd heard the news that The Altruistic Traveller herself was venturing there. Some invited me to visit their projects, others offered to host me in exchange for a write-up of their stories. It seemed that, despite my modesty surrounding the blog and the advocacy I'd devoted in 2016, The Altruistic Traveller had become a well-known name in the social-impact scene.

Preparing to leave Australia was also much less unnerving than my previous *bon voyage*. My friends and family were unsurprised by the news, just simply happy that I was following a path that felt true to who I was. I had noticed a shift in myself as well, whereby I was starting to steadily embody this version of me – the unconventional girl who lived an unconventional life. I was not yet her though; there was still a way to go to reprogram myself out of thirty-one years of societal conditioning. But I had made headway.

About a week before my departure date, I received a text message from Dean. "I'd like to see you before you go," it read. "Let's meet Friday at Wendy's Secret Garden."

I had broken the news to him about my intended departure a few days prior despite our decision to press pause on our relationship. His genuine response was unsurprising. It seemed fitting to be in his tender presence at another significant turning point in my life. He seemed to appear, like a guardian angel, at these times of great relevance. Even when he was not physically by my side, he was there. He was always there.

That Friday, I rode the Illawarra train from the southern suburbs of Sydney, took my usual change at Town Hall station to platform three, and then hopped on the T1-North Shore line to North Sydney. I'd taken that journey hundreds of times and the dazzling views of Sydney Harbour, with the Opera House as its centrepiece, never failed to prompt a faint nostalgia while the train chugged along the 85-year-old railway, across the iconic Harbour Bridge. Sydney is a gorgeous city.

Wendy's Secret Garden is a rare oasis beneath the sprawling high-rises of Sydney's second-largest business district. There is something magical about nature reserves inside cities. They are sanctuaries: a refuge to breathe and slow down while chaos danced around you. Each time I walked down the stairs descending into that oasis, I felt like I was walking into an enchanted forest, as though I was a character in Fern Gully about to be nurtured and protected by the magic of Mother Nature herself. Colourful flora like lavender, clivias and hydrangeas complement the lush hues of green that engulf the garden. A giant Moreton Bay Fig tree towers over them all, like a sculptural grandmother.

Dean and I sat at the table beneath the fig tree. That was our usual spot. It offered an uninterrupted view all the way out to the Sydney Harbour Bridge, atop the silhouettes of palms and plumeria. On a clear blue-sky day, like that day, the image was a postcard. That picture always felt familiar to me.

"Even though it's hard for me to watch you leave again, I feel like this is the right move for you. You shine out there, from what I can see," Dean said, as we stared out at the azure sky.

"Thank you," I replied. "It's hard for me to leave here, to leave you, but Nepal is going to be good for me. I can feel it. I wish there was a way to have you there with me."

"Well, you know what would happen if I did come with you? We'd break the space-time continuum. And who knows what would happen then," he said, trying to evoke a smile, as he always did.

I let out a moderate laugh.

"Fine, let's break it!" I said, accompanied by a melancholic smile.

It was becoming apparent to me that the love story between Dean and I was not linear. The more I let go of expecting it to be traditional, the more acceptance I found for what it was – enigmatic and fluid, like water. In many ways, all relationships are this way. Yet, we attempt to solidify them, like ice cubes, in a freezer of our own and others' expectations. We don't keep people. There is no "you are mine and I am yours." There is no "you complete me." We are individual mortal bodies with immortal souls walking together through this existence making conscious, and unconscious, decisions every single moment that define our story, our legacy. We can love one another, inspire one another and influence one another, but ultimately, the paths we walk are ours.

If that scene of my life were a Hollywood movie, Dean or I would have most likely begged the other to stay, got down on one knee, declared our love and said something like, "I can't live without you." Or, one of us would have hastily grabbed a taxi to the airport and stood at the boarding gates with flowers or a string quartet playing Ed Sheeran in the background, followed by "Don't leave me" or "I'm coming with you." But that wasn't how the scripts played out in real life. And that wasn't unconditional love.

Love is finding happiness in the happiness of another. It is smiling when they accomplish something important to them. It is listening intently to their unfeigned words and the messages within. It is holding space while they share their deepest thoughts and dreams. It is not trying to change them or halt their growth, even if it means enduring the suffering that occurs when our hearts ache. In all our years together, Dean never tried to change me. Instead, he selflessly reminded me to use my wings and fly.

I tilted my head to the right side and gently leaned it on his shoulder. We both sat in silence looking out at a symbol of a city that brought us together on that sweet day back in July 2014. I had changed so much since then. The world had changed. But one thing remained the same – the love I held, so deeply, for the man sitting beside me, beneath the shade of the ficus tree.

"You'll always be in my heart," he said. "I love you, unconditionally."

Chapter 19 - Kathmandu

From the vantage point of a common balcony in an austere hostel in Thamel, I gazed towards a setting sun that hid behind a purple haze, blanketing the jagged edges of the red-clay-brick buildings and concrete rooftops that sprawled across the basin of Kathmandu. Nepal's capital city sits within a low-lying valley that geological and fossil evidence indicates was, historically, a great lake. Once teeming with fish, is now teeming with pedestrians, rickshaws, cars and tooting motorbikes. From the outside in, the city appears disorderly, but from the inside out, Kathmandu is enchanting. And as I watched the glaring sun trickle behind the Nagarjun forest, I had begun to fall under its spell.

Earlier that week, I met the woman who influenced my journey to Nepal. The Local Women's Handicrafts shopfront was an eight-minute walk from my hostel, through the rutted streets of Kathmandu's popular tourist district. Thamel is a condensed assembly of guesthouses, eateries, bars, outlets, supermarkets, and any of the other fit-for-purpose merchants who thought to benefit from the city's main tourist thoroughfare. The density of the buildings fringing the single-lane streets warrants a no-car-zone, but frequent cars and motorcycles maneuver past regardless, lawlessly honking their horns at the occasional rickshaw rider pedalling cumbersomely as he carries the weight of two bodies on his rickety tricycle.

The hues of coloured threads, woven into merchandise like t-shirts and handbags that hung on display outside the shopfronts lining the narrow streets, contrasted the craggy, concrete buildings and sooty tarmac. Many of the stores flaunted a familiar assortment of products: hemp bags, mara beads, singing bowls, prayer wheels, prayer flags, pashminas, woollen hats, woollen gloves, hiking boots, camping gear, and basically anything one would need to either keep warm in the high altitudes of the Himalayas or take home an embossed representation of one's time in Nepal. As with any main tourist passage, consumerism was exploited, and it wasn't any different there on the streets of Thamel. However, as I strolled through the artery of materialism, on my way to meet a victim of child sweatshop labour and start my volunteer placement to assist with advocacy for greater transparency and human rights in the textiles industry, I couldn't help but ask myself, who made these products?

I turned left onto Paknajol Marg, emerging from the bazaar that was Z Street, and followed Google Maps' navigation arrow like Pacman, eating every blue dot until I reached the Local Women's Handicrafts store. There, on my right, was a glass-pane storefront with two tables outside. One displaying multicoloured shawls folded tidily on top of one another, and the other displaying satchels, delicately embroidered with spiral and floral patterns. The sign atop the glass windowpane read, 'Handmade Products By Women's Group.' Beneath those words were three phrases: '100% fair trade', '100% fair price', 'Empower one another through skills.' My mind was transported back to the Zoom call with Nasreen. This was the place, I thought. *This was the place that changed her life forever.*

As I entered the shopfront, a young woman approached me. Her skin was soft and brown, her hair dark like night.

"Hi," I smiled, shyly. "I'm looking for Nasreen."

"Hello!" the young woman said. "She will be here in a few minutes. If you like, you can take a look around our store while you wait."

The store was colourful and compact, filled with positive affirmations that spoke to the values Nasreen embodied in her communications with me. To my left, on a wall that displayed a range of decorative costume jewellery, a sign read, 'Your purchase makes a difference'. Above me, a crinkled, handwritten piece of paper stuck to the wall with a green push pin read, 'Help us to empower women'. I scanned the range of products before me. My eyes fixated on an embroidered rug, flaunting all the colours of the rainbow. I leaned in closer to read the label.

Local Women's Handicrafts is a fair trade sewing collective based out of Kathmandu, Nepal, that focuses on empowering and educating disadvantaged women. We do this by providing paid training programs in design, sewing, weaving, embroidery, knitting, jewellery-making and pattern work. This traditional, handmade rug is woven using recycled silk from discarded saris, which have been collected and repurposed. Your purchase of a single rug helps everyone involved in this project strengthen their lives in Nepal.

Suddenly, I felt very connected to the people whose hands wove that rug.

My perusing was interrupted by a silvery voice.

"Bianca? Hello!"

I turned around to see Nasreen walking towards me. Both her attire and manner were vibrant. It was as though she radiated at least three-and-a-half feet in every direction. She was wearing a teal kurta with white printed feathers atop cobalt blue harem pants. A pastel-coloured shawl draped lightly over her dark hair and across her chest.

"Hi," I said, as I walked closer to her, allured by her radiance.

We leaned in for a hug that felt the way you would embrace a close friend you hadn't seen in a long time. It was as though we already knew each other – two visionary light-workers colliding like energised electrons to strengthen their force. It is remarkable the power that can be generated when like-minded souls find one another, in lightness or in dark.

"It's so nice to finally meet you," Nasreen said. "And I see you've met my sister, Sahin, too."

"You too," I replied. "It's so lovely to meet you both."

"We'll head to the centre in a minute. It's about a thirty-minute drive from here depending on the traffic. I'll call a taxi," she said.

The Local Women's Handicrafts centre was located in the village of Goldhunga which sat on a hillside beneath the Nagarjun forest. It was the headquarters for the social enterprise and the space where most of the products found in the store were created.

Our white Suzuki hatchback taxi, which looked to have reached its prime back in the early nineties, weaved in and out of Kathmandu's traffic, ascending out of the low-lying smog and towards clearer skies. Once we entered the village via the main road, the driver turned down an uneven dirt track, transforming our ride into a bumpy journey.

We pulled up to a half-completed three-storey building that overlooked the Kathmandu Valley. A large, dark green, wrought iron gate guarded the entrance to the ground level. In the taxi ride over, Nasreen had explained to me that the centre was a work in progress: a dream forming, depending on the funds that she was able to accrue.

"We bought the land in 2012," she explained. "In 2013, we built the foundations and the first floor and then spent eighteen months working from two basic rooms. We acquired more funding in 2015 to continue the build, but the earthquake happened in April and so that year, this place became a facility to distribute aid to the community."

According to United Nations' metrics, in 2016, Nepal was one of the least developed countries in Asia. Its geographic location in one of the most disaster-prone regions on Earth, coupled with challenging topography, contributed to this ranking. Economic matters worsened on 25 April 2015, when a 7.8 magnitude earthquake struck just northwest of the capital of Kathmandu. It was the worst earthquake in the region in more than eighty years. Nearly 9,000 lives were lost and over 600,000 homes were destroyed. It was a time when the world turned to Nepal, but it was the people there, on the ground, that were ultimately left to tackle the challenging clean-up. People, like Nasreen and the women she worked with, banded together to provide support in whichever ways they could as they raced against the clock to reach the country's most vulnerable.

"We ate, we lived, we worked, and we distributed assistance packages from this centre. It was a challenging time, but also an example of the comradery and kind-heartedness of the Nepalese people," she said.

I disembarked from the Suzuki hatchback and walked towards the gate. It stood taller than I, so I couldn't see what lay beyond, but I could hear the faint voices of women speaking in Nepali.

"We keep this gate here for security," Nasreen explained. "Some people in the community don't agree with the level of autonomy we have created for the women and so we try to protect them as much as possible."

The plight of gender equality in Nepal is complex. Deep-rooted, patriarchal cultural norms situate men, both traditionally and legislatively, above women in most aspects of Nepalese culture. And while slow progress is emerging in cities like Kathmandu – where life is slightly more progressive – rural Nepal tells a very different story of women. In rural areas, women are subject to inequalities such as lack of decision-making opportunities, lack of access to land and property rights, child marriages, stigmatisation of widows and divorcees (which perpetuates family violence), segregation of women and girls during menstruation (*chhaupadi*), and fewer opportunities to work outside the home without being outcast by their immediate circles.

These ideologies have become so normal that many women never knew any alternative and, in turn, preserve inequality by silently yielding to its existence. For these women, speaking out against the social norm denotes the difference between being accepted by others or ostracised. Even Nasreen's mother disapproved of her defying espousal of female empowerment, labelling her an "embarrassment and shame" to the family.

You may be surprised at how one's own mother could not be proud of a woman like Nasreen, but I understood, having been through a similar personal experience. I witnessed how indoctrination and entrenched belief systems can blind people who become deluded by a veil of subjectivism that inhibits their ability to love without attached conditions. The human mind, as malleable as it is, is hard to recondition once beliefs become a calcified part of one's identity – especially, when the very act of critical thinking could threaten one's fundamental need for acceptance.

A woman opened the gate from the inside. She wore a scarlet red kurta and a contagious smile. As I entered the foyer, another woman approached me. She was holding a brass round tray, with canary-yellow marigold flowers dispersed among a lit flame and a small mound of red powder.

"This is a tika blessing," Nasreen said. "Tika is a common tradition in Hinduism. The mixture is made from dried turmeric and placed on the sixth chakra. It signifies a deep blessing to the individual on whom it is placed."

I stood in front of the woman. Her dark eyes, the tops outlined by a faultless streak of black eyeliner, complemented by perfectly threaded eyebrows, stared into mine as she placed her thumb into the mound and then gently smeared a small amount of tika on my forehead.

"*Namasté*," she said.

"Namasté," I replied as I placed my hands into prayer and bowed slightly.

The word "namasté" was derived from the old Sanskrit language found in the ancient Veda texts. In English, it translates to, "I bow to the divine in you." It was a word and a symbol that would appear almost daily during my time in Nepal; a word that would come to mean so much to me.

As I greeted the seven women in the room, all dressed in the most vivid colours of the visible spectrum, my eyes were compelled to a large mural painted on the back wall beside a hallway that led to the production rooms. Between animated floral paintings of beaming yellow, blue, and green were the hand-painted words, "Strength lies in differences not in similarities." The centre felt like a sanctuary. It emanated empowerment and I could sense from the women I met that they felt safe there.

While visiting that day, I was offered a short tour of the property. I was guided through the ground floor of the main building, past the embroidery and cutting rooms, and then out into the garden via a vegetable patch in the surrounding lawn.

Nasreen shared with me some of the sustainability initiatives she and her team had implemented at the centre, including an underground water storage tank with two months' water supply for emergencies, biogas for cooking, and solar panels for heating. In some ways, those premises were more environmentally efficient than many of the Australian homes I grew up in.

Beyond the gardens, we entered a large shed. Inside contained eight wooden looms, all more than a metre in width and traditionally crafted for the weaving of raw materials. Five women were working that day, preparing the materials and weaving the Local Women's Handicrafts' signature product: recycled sari rugs. They greeted me with smiles as Nasreen guided me through the premises and shared more about the production process.

"We gather discarded materials from the local community and repurpose them, so they don't end up in a landfill. We have a natural dying process where we extract colours from plants and leaves, and we use a thousand-year-old technique to turn raw materials into yarn, which we weave through a hundred-year-old loom that doesn't require electricity," she explained.

I was captivated as I watched the women work. One woman was sorting a pile of striking fabrics that shone beneath the dappled sunlight and illuminated out of the corner of my eye from whatever spot I stood inside that shed. One woman sorted the various reels of thread that stood on the concrete floor like scattered tiny termite mounds. The others confidently sat behind their composite century-old looms, fluently weaving inch-wide pieces of the recycled materials together to create something both old and new – a transformed masterpiece with an opportunity for a new life, much like the opportunities of the women whose hands wove them. Nasreen's progressive commitment to sustainability never ceased to amaze me. I hoped her advocacy would have a ripple effect on a nation vulnerable to climate change impacts.

It was important for a country like Nepal – which hadn't yet succumbed to the consumer-driven plague that continues to relentlessly exploit our planet for every last resource – to consider implementing practices that deter the country from further environmental degradation at the hands of capitalism. They have a word for this in the international development arena: leapfrogging. Essentially, it means that perceptibly lesser developed nations would "leapfrog" over the stages of development of more perceptibly developed nations – specifically, the stages of development that disregarded the conservation of the natural world.

The proverbial expression "necessity is the mother of invention" rang true in cases where countries like Nepal were asked to compensate for the destruction perpetuated by more wasteful and energy consuming nations, like China and the United States. I bore witness to incredible grassroots organisations like Clean City which were implementing innovative solutions in waste management and water security. Or Conscious Impact, who aided in regenerative agricultural initiatives, such as coffee, permaculture design, and agroforestry. Their work was becoming increasingly necessary in the fragile ecosystem of Nepal.

Nepal has a high rural population of roughly eighty percent, meaning many of the nation's inhabitants still live off the land, intrinsically connected to the climate conditions of the Himalayan altitudes. I recall sleeping in a homestay in the village of Manikhel, situated about 40 kilometres south of Kathmandu. I was hosted by Hirameya, or "Ani" as I would call her (*ani* means aunt in Nepalese). She lived on a hillside village in a small Tamang community, one of the largest Tibeto-Burman ethnic groups in Nepal. Fresh spring water flowed from the mountains, through irrigation pipes and down into the village, nourishing the fertile land. I remember picking cabbages and carrots with Ani's niece, Indra, who accompanied me during my stay, helping to translate the dialogue between Ani and me. We used those garden ingredients as stuffing for the *momos* and curry components for *dal bhat*. If we needed milk for our *chiya*, we would walk five minutes to the neighbour's home to collect a churn of milk from the buffalo they kept. There was no need for a thirty-aisle supermarket full of packaged, preservative-ridden, often unnecessary, commodities. In Nepal, and every other corner of this earth, the land provides and deserves to be protected.

"It's getting late," I heard Nasreen's voice over the sound of women's laughter. "Let's go back to Kathmandu. I have a bit of work to finish off."

We farewelled the women at the centre and gathered outside of the building.

"I can't get a hold of a taxi," Nasreen said. "Let's walk to the top of the road and see if we can get one there."

We ascended the inclined, potholed road. An uninterrupted view of the Kathmandu Basin spread behind us. It was peaceful there, on that hill. A Himalayan silence soothed me. It distracted me during the time we waited for a taxi to pass until the sound of a harsh engine drew near.

A navy-blue truck slowed down and approached us. Nasreen muttered some words in Nepali to the driver who casually hung out the open window.

"I guess this is our ride," she said. "Hop in."

This? I thought to myself as I hesitantly followed her to the back of the truck.

I mimicked Nasreen and grabbed the top hatch of the truck's tray container to pull myself up onto the back ledge and then stepped into the load tray – an unlikely piece of cargo. The floor was covered in a layer tan clay dust too thick to bother wiping the surface down before I sat on it.

I looked at Nasreen. We were both laughing at our rather incautious escapade. As the truck chugged along the dirt road, dust particles fell upon us like a sun shower. I covered my hair with a reliable shawl I had purchased many years ago from a street vendor in Jaipur. That brightly hued shawl travelled everywhere with me. It converted into a make-do blanket, as well as a decent mask to protect me from the smog of Jaipur and now, the dust of Kathmandu.

"This is Nepal," she said as we both clung tightly to the sides of the cargo tray-turned taxi.

I arrived back at the hostel in time for another sublime sunset from the common area on the rooftop. As I walked in the direction of my six-bed female dorm, through the dimly lit lobby, with walls covered in travel posters advertising trekking guides and onward journeys to Bhutan or India, and up the stairs to the second floor, I heard distant echoes of chatter coming from the rooftop. I had noticed a few additional pairs of trekking shoes outside the doors that lined the hallways. Some new housemates have arrived, I thought to myself.

It had been a long and adventurous day. After long days, I tended to retreat to the most solitary place I could find, like a hermit crab scuttling backwards into the confines of its shelled home. But that day, I took a shower to remove the dust particles that attached to my skin, like matte foundation, tied my long, brown hair into a loose bun atop my head, and ascended the three floors to the balcony that overlooked Kathmandu.

"Hola!"

The sound of a young man's voice triggered some of the people at the table to gaze with intrigue in my direction, examining the party's newcomer.

"Hi," I replied. "Mind if I join you?"

"All are welcome here. We are *inclusivo!*" said the man.

I pulled up a chair at the long white plastic table that sat at the centre of the balcony beneath a dusking sky. Five people shared the area. Two, slightly segregated and engaged in their own conversation, and three others, who I sat with.

"We're just in the middle of a conversation about energy and the quantum field," the man said as he proceeded to pull a cigarette from the packet that sat on the table beneath a tall bottle of condensing Gorkha Strong.

"I was sharing an experience I recently had, whereby I thought about someone I hadn't spoken to in years, and they contacted me the following morning. Have you experienced that phenomenon?" he asked.

"Actually, yes. Many times," I replied.

"Ah! You have the gift too," he said.

"Could be a coincidence," said another man, sitting opposite me to the left. "But there are scientific studies that continue to dive deeper into atoms and electrons and this whole quantum physics stuff," he said.

"I like to call it magic," I responded, placing my sincere opinion down on the invisible deck of transcendental, theoretical cards we had stacked between us. "I believe we have more senses than just the notable five. But most of the time they're either shrugged off as nonsense or turned into some religious doctrine."

"Ella cree en la magia!" said the man to my right as he adjusted the black Detroit Tigers cap he was wearing. "My kind of human."

"I'm Tyler by the way. And this is Daniel," he said, pointing his right arm gently across the table in the direction of his friend and then shifting his chair a few degrees toward me so he was facing slightly more aligned with my paracentral vision. "We met this evening."

"I'm Bianca. Nice to meet you. And thank you for this intriguing discussion. You seem to have a hunch about the topics I'm interested in."

"Nepal has a way of bringing people like us together," Tyler said. "You'll see what I mean once you spend some time here."

I felt unexpectedly relaxed for a first-time encounter with three strangers. We didn't start our introductions with the typical "Where are you from?" or "What do you do?." All those questions seemed rather irrelevant, superficial. It was as though we existed beyond that place. Somewhere deeper.

Hours passed that evening without one glance at the time, beneath the basalt blanket of a Kathmandu sky that reflected city lights. I was mesmerised by the inspiration and intrigue that grew in every word we spoke inside our circle of collective curiosity. We spoke of time and the illusion of it, parallel universes, our deepest pains and how we were guided to overcome them, love, truth, destiny. *How did I find myself here? Spellbound? What was it about this place that had enveloped me so?*

The rare hush of Kathmandu approached us in the early hours of that morning. The table beneath us was scattered with empty Sherpa Brewery cans, an ashtray full of cigarettes, and a lone red cellophane lighter that may or may not have found a new home that night.

"I like the word 'inclusivo'," I said to Tyler, as I stared over at him slouching back in his chair, gazing at the few stars visible in the night sky. His neutral skin reflected the white light of a makeshift lamp we had assembled in the middle of the table using the torch function of my mobile phone and standing up against an empty beer bottle. The silhouette of a pair of Bose headphones wrapped around his neck.

"It means to be inclusive, right?"

"*Si,*" he replied.

186

"I like to make sure people feel included too – that they feel safe in my presence and are able to speak, without judgement. It's something I appreciate in the spaces I find myself in."

"You're empathic. I can sense it," he said. "I am too. We feel. We create. We notice things. It's who we are."

"It is," I responded, my vulnerability creeping to the surface the more at ease I felt in his presence. "It just means, for me at least, the world can feel a little overwhelming at times. It's like, I feel more than I see. And because of that, I dance between wanting to keep myself safe and wanting to shine."

"You shine, honey. Don't dim your radiant light. You've got so much to give this world," he said with conviction in his tone.

I'd often reflected on whether my immense sensitivity to the world around me was a strength or a weakness. On days I carried the weight of others' suffering like a thorn in my side, I'd paradoxically covet apathy. *What would it feel like to not feel?* But then, I'd be reminded that I didn't have that choice. The ability to deeply feel was a gene forged into my DNA, like the colour of the roots of my hair. So, instead, I was called to use that gene, like the abilities of an X-men character, and leverage it: learn to use it, control it and, ultimately, embrace a love for it. Once I was able to change my perspective on this part of myself, it no longer fell into the category of weakness or strength. It became a gift.

"Can I teach you another word in Spanish?" Tyler asked, as marble-like waves of cigarette smoke danced above his aura.

"Of course," I replied.

"*Alma*," he said. "It means soul."

I smiled. A tender, gentle sensation came upon me, causing the tiny hair follicles on my arms to contract.

"That's a special word," I said. "I'll remember that."

"Thank you for being a *conexión del alma* tonight," he said.

"Thank you for being inclusivo," I replied.

We looked at each other and let out a collective bout of laughter. That was the night I experienced the powerful, spiritual magnetism of the Himalayas, that lures in valiant and deviant pilgrims like bumble bees to lavender flowers.

Chapter 20 - Inside out

After some weeks in Kathmandu, it had become apparent to me that Nepal was rich in spirituality and held deeply devout roots. Each morning, as I began my daily routine, I would walk beneath the presence of colourful prayer flags. They were situated in abundance atop laneways, over storefronts, and throughout the interior of most restaurants in Thamel, including the garden of the Revolution Café I frequented most mornings, draped between the branches of a palm tree that shaded the outdoor dining tables. Despite being a majority Hindu nation, the presence of Buddhist prayer flags was somewhat of a national symbol in Nepal. They were the rainbow umbrella of Kathmandu, an emblem representing faith and devotion.

Throughout those earlier weeks in Nepal, while finding my feet and culinary discretions, I'd begun to collate a list of preferential hangouts: Western Tandoori Naan House for the most affordable nosh in town; The Café With No Name for chocolate chip muffins, reasonable Wi-Fi speeds and a quaint reading lounge; The Momo Hut for my Nepalese dumpling (also known as momo) fix; and OR2K, a popular franchise serving arguably some of the best Middle-Eastern cuisines outside of the Middle East. Many of those more socially minded eateries, like OR2K, placed community boards at their entrances. The boards were often pinned to the brim with pamphlets advertising yoga retreats, reiki classes, meditation classes, tai chi, singing bowl lessons, and a number of other practices that afforded individuals the opportunity to take a journey within.

At the time, I'd steadily begun to explore the contents of my inner world, dipping my toes into a lake or a sea of unknown size. That year I spent backpacking through Southeast Asia helped me become closer to myself. It stripped away some of the layers that no longer served me, parts of an identity I had created from conformity, as opposed to authenticity. The sheer ability for me to be present for almost a whole year, undistracted by incessant demands, opened up the space for inner exploration. That, coupled with an unabating curiosity about what the mainstream population ironically labelled 'new age', led me to practices like yoga and meditation. Little did I know that being in Nepal was going to be my initiation into deeper practice – my red pill.

It was a common trait of mine to adapt into my surroundings. Each time I found myself at a destination, I'd develop the skills of the chameleon, influenced by what was around me. Whenever I stepped off the aeroplane in London, I'd find myself walking at least two times faster than my average walking pace. When I was in the USA, I'd start to pronounce my r's (which was uncommon for Australians, whose pronunciation of water was more like 'woor-da'). When in India, it wasn't too long before my 'yes' response was accompanied by a subtle head wobble. So naturally, when in Nepal, my chameleon response propelled my spiritual curiosity even further.

I took some photographs of the pinned pamphlets that caught my attention on the community board: the weekly timetable for two local yoga studios, a meditation retreat in Pokhara, a volunteer placement in the country's north, and a Tibetan singing bowl workshop. There were so many activities, I had to refrain from option paralysis and attune to what felt achievable for me during my stay, while also working and assisting the women at the centre.

I soon found a routine that allowed me to balance my inner exploration and my prior obligations. I'd wake up before 7 am, dress for the day and then take my laptop to one of three cafés that were open early for breakfast, and that had a decent Wi-Fi connection. If it wasn't the Revolution Café, or the Café With No Name, I'd head to Nepal Connection on the popular Mandala Street. Despite the café's prime location, I was the only one there most mornings. One morning, however, I was not alone. On that particular day, at that particular hour, there was a man sitting on the couches nearby the charging station where I would need to charge my laptop. He had a long main of frosty hair, tied neatly in a ponytail, and wore an unironed, orange t-shirt with a tattered image of a blue Shiva in the centre of the chest. I sat at a table opposite him. We exchanged a fleeting look of kind acknowledgement but nothing more. I turned my gaze toward my laptop screen and commenced my work.

That day had started off as any other, except an invisible sadness lingered around me as I struggled to come to terms with my feelings about Dean. Grief often seems to fall into the category of death, but it can be found in life too. The grief of a relationship ending, of losing someone you loved who is still on this earthly plane, or the loss of a love story you could have had, is very much real. We grieve the possibility. And I grieved the possibility of him, of having him with me, just like I had dreamed of all those years ago.

I ordered my daily cup of tea from the sweet waitress who always greeted me with a smile.

"You're American?" I heard the man's voice from across the table.

"Australian actually," I replied. My Australian accent faded a little when I travelled. I was left with a concoction of accents and pronunciations accumulated through discussions with people from all over the world.

"Where are you from?" I replied.

"Murwillumbah, near Byron Bay," he responded.

Although I perceived borders to be quite arbitrary, there is an immediate bond that forms when you cross paths with someone from the same country or region as you. It is an instinctive familiarity, almost tribal.

"My name is Jayavada," he said.

"Jayavada is a very unique name. Where is that from?"

"It's a long story," he said. "It came to me many years ago in a meditation."

My mind highlighted the word "meditation" with a fluorescent yellow marker. Although I felt like an amateur in the practice, I was deeply intrigued by its power. Not only for myself but for the whole world. Hearing the word triggered my deeper attention. It notified me that this man and I were on the same wavelength. I thought about Tyler's words: 'Nepal has a way of bringing people like us together …'

"I'll call you Jai," I responded, attempting to shield myself from mispronouncing his name.

"What brings you to this part of the world?" I asked, holding the warm mug of lemon and ginger tea in my hands and receiving a faint scent of lemongrass in the evaporating steam.

"I'm working with the owner of this café, Mahabir Pun. We're distributing laptops to schools in remote regions of Nepal."

I would come to learn that the Nepal Connection café was, in fact, a social enterprise, with profits from the restaurant supporting education and health programs in rural Nepal. Like Siem Reap, Kathmandu was a hub for socially innovative projects that contributed to wider social and economic development throughout the country.

"That's a beautiful cause. I'd love to support you in any way I can. I write about social impact projects like this."

"Thank you, Bianca," he replied, sincerely.

Jai and I went on to talk about many things that morning in the café, all of which held great significance to the emotions I was feeling at the time. I never brought up how I was feeling about my recent separation from Dean, yet the conversation continuously diverted towards topics of the self, attachment, love and what it meant to be human. It's as if all the questions I had in my mind were being answered by this mysterious individual sitting opposite me on that sunny morning in May.

"There is something I'd like to tell you," Jai said, in the midst of our ethereal dialogue. "I'm getting a feeling and a message to tell you this. Is that ok?"

"Of course," I replied. "I'm open to receiving the message."

"I sense a sadness in you," he said, as he looked into my eyes with a gentle focus. "And I want to tell you that everything is going to be OK."

He paused. Perhaps for a few seconds but to me, it felt longer than that. I concentrated on him. Everything around me blurred. Not even a pesky fly could grab my attention in those moments.

"Your sadness is just a lesson in perception. There is something for you to learn, Bianca."

He continued, "We can't go through this life without the emotion of sadness because we would never grow. In its polarity, the emotion is as perfect as happiness. It is here to offer us a perspective, to help us on our journey of becoming. Those who choose to ignore or suppress sadness will just find it again and again until it eventually consumes them. Feel through it. The universe speaks to us in experiences and helps us to heal through emotions. That is the divine language."

His words pierced me. Every single one. I felt tears well in my eyes. I felt held – seen. *Was I dreaming? Was this all real? How did this man know I needed to hear those words?*

My thoughts sometimes take me back to that morning in the café and I wonder if it was a dream. I never saw Jai again after that. Like many of the people that move through our lives in exquisite timing, perhaps that was the single purpose of our souls' encounter.

I'd grown to believe that there was a meaning behind every unique moment in our lives. Call it fate, call it synchronicity, call it dreaming, but this life – this whole existence – was a miracle in itself. If we were lucky, we lived a billion fleeting moments, intricately pieced together like dominoes, impacting each other, one second after the next. I couldn't explain why Jai and I met in the café that morning. But that afternoon, on my way to a vinyasa yoga class, I pondered on the message he shared with me like Indiana Jones trying to locate the Holy Grail. *What was the sadness teaching me?*

I entered the space of the Charak Yoga Studio on Chaksibari Marg. There was a peaceful essence to the room. It felt like a sanctuary within the bustling capital of Kathmandu. The class was barely full, with just three other women seated on their mats facing the hand-painted mandala on the front wall of the studio. A man approached me. We greeted each other with a *"namasté"* and a slight bow, our palms together in prayer.

He paused for a moment and gazed into my eyes.

"Have you been here before?" he said. "Your face is very familiar."

"It's my first time in Nepal actually," I replied.

"Must have been another life then," he said in a jovial tone. "Make yourself comfortable. We will start in a moment."

I sat in the middle row of yoga mats. I wasn't one to sit at the front. Not in a yoga class or in any other kind of group setting. The further away, the less likely I'd feel judged – an unconscious habit from my bashful childhood. Kanchan sat cross-legged at the front of the studio. His essence made me feel that he had been practising yoga for a long time, although he was still quite young, perhaps in his late thirties or early forties. He spoke gently, yet with assertiveness and a fine knowledge of the asanas.

The vinyasa practice that day was intermediate. The stiffness in my body unveiled the muscular tension gripping my emotional pain, worry and fears like unkempt vines of English ivy. I'd learned more about the mind-body connection in recent years than I had ever learned in any of my primary or secondary education, or in my school of life. It wasn't until anxiety consumed me that day in the corporate slammer, that I learned about stress being one of the leading causes of physical illness in Western societies. Adversely, the foundational model of Western society was designed to keep people in that stressful state, so they continued to remain useful pawns on a capitalistic chess board devised in a way that only the tycoons could win. *Drink this alcohol*, they said. *Eat this junk food*, they said. *Smoke these cigarettes*, they said. *Fill the void in your heart with this brand new Fendi bag, it will make you feel gorgeous*, they said. **Disclaimer, dopamine rushes may only last 24 hours. We are not responsible for any human rights violations that may have occurred in the manufacturing process of these products.*

Yoga was, at least, one kind of moderately esoteric exercise that enticed the mainstream individual. I was glad it sprung to popularity in recent decades, even if it was influenced by West Hollywood soccer mums in Lululemon activewear and sundered from its sacred Vedic origins. Savasana (the pose at the end of the practice where the body is invited to rest) could have arguably been, for some, the longest form of respite outside of a good night's sleep. It is one of the best parts of the practice. Lying down, drifting away. A loose, tired body, too relaxed to think a multitude of thoughts about a past we cannot change and a future we have not yet met.

I lay on the mat, feeling my body connected to the floor below. My legs and arms were extended, resting comfortably at my sides. My palms faced up. Calming, instrumental music sang around me, drifting me into a deeper state of consciousness, like an elevator going farther and farther down a shaft, away from the noise, away from the chaos. I felt my body become lighter, as light as a feather. It was as though the floor and I were no longer separate. The sound of my heartbeat slowed until it was a distant echo of vibration. My mind was still, like the silence between breaths. There was an inexplicable peace in that place I drifted to, a place where everything and nothing collided.

The soft chime of a bell brought me back.

"Very slowly and very gently, begin to make small movements with your fingers and your toes," Kanchan's voice met my ears.

My body was still airy, but my mind was there, back in Kathmandu, firing the neurons that spoke to the nerves in my hands and feet. I sat up slowly, feeling at least two kilograms lighter than when I walked into that studio. I'd gifted myself rest – radical presence. My body held gratitude. I could feel it.

There is a truth to the solace one can find when accessing the silence within. I'd felt it now. And after that day in the studio, the practice of meditation became my private, sacred temple with a door that was always open.

Chapter 21 - Awakening

Those months in Nepal transformed me in more ways than I could have ever imagined. If I wasn't in the field with Nasreen and the women, I was descending my internal staircase, accessing and unlocking rooms in my subconscious. Each meditation practice helped me to find the stillness required to meet myself on a deeper level. There was much wisdom to be found in the silence of that stillness, and once I'd learned how to access it, I became an explorer of the wilderness within. It helped that I was nurtured by the collective energy of the Himalayas, being a stone's throw away from ancient holy shrines like Swayambhunaath Temple and Boudhanath Stupa. Perhaps my chameleon superpowers are just a by-product of a collective consciousness that permeates the social pockets of our vast world. If laughter is contagious, if seeing someone in a state of sadness makes us upset too, then who's to say that me walking two times faster than my average walking pace in London isn't representative of a frazzled collective in a constant state of relentless productivity? Could it be possible that the energy we emanate influences those around us more than we understand? And if so, what would happen if the whole world entered a peaceful state of a billion savasanas?

One afternoon, I accompanied two friends I met at the hostel, Raluca and Helge, on a day trip to the nearby Pashupatinath Temple. Raluca and Helge were resolute travellers like me, and so the thought of catching one of the local microbuses, as ratty and overcrowded as they were, wasn't misgiving. Kathmandu's microbuses were an affordable transport option that connected the thronging city with surrounding villages. The four-kilometre journey to Pashupatinath Temple would set you back about 25 Nepalese rupees (roughly 20 cents). The white or blue minibuses claimed to have a maximum capacity, but that was patently redundant. Commuters fit into every last crevice of those steel containers like tinned sardines, and so did we.

I held on tightly to the railing above me, Raluca to my left and Helge in front of us. The sheer density of the crowd meant that even around a bend there was nowhere to fall. We just pressed up against one another's arms like ravers in a mosh pit. We stopped behind a long line of cars. In the far distance, I could see a set of traffic lights. There was traffic congestion everywhere. I could barely make out the road beneath all the vehicles. For a while, the bus wasn't making any ground. I stood there, leaning on the back of Helge's navy-blue shirt, patterned with white Sanskrit symbols. He smelt like the juxtaposing concoction of tobacco and palo santo, a sacred tree whose wood is used in traditional healing and spiritual ceremonies. I liked the smell of palo santo; it had a calming essence to it and it matched Helge's aura. He was a gentle soul born in Nepal to German parents and deeply connected to the magic of that land.

I looked up at the traffic lights again. They had changed from green to red three times and we hadn't moved at all. I felt agitation rise in my body like an hourglass in reverse. I felt impatient. My mind started to spiral. *What if we just walked? Couldn't the driver find a faster way? What if we got off the bus and tried to get a taxi instead?* In those moments, all I wanted was to escape the reality I was in, change it somehow. The erratic thought process exacerbated my agitation, consuming me from the inside out. I looked around at the other people on the bus. They were simply standing there, patiently, in silence. Breathing. Waiting. *How was no one else on this bus as frustrated as I was?* If I was in Sydney, there'd be a rumpus. I could hear it in my mind. 'I want to speak to the manager in charge. This is unacceptable,' they would say. Yet there I was, surrounded by people in a pacified presence. And then I stopped for a moment. I stopped thinking about all the ways I could get myself out of that situation. What did it matter if we moved through the traffic lights there and then, or at a time in the future? Why was I trying to control the outcome? That obsessive and amplified need for control was of no benefit to me or anyone around me.

The conditioning I exhibited from years of growing up in a society on a constant hamster wheel showed in subtle ways, like that day on the bus in Nepal. There was a mind-heaviness to the culture I grew up in. It seemed like we were always asked to live in our heads: to think, to plan, to examine and, ultimately, to control. In those prior years, I began to challenge the narrative of leading with the mind. I learned that our bodies are capable of so much more; to *feel*, to *trust*; to be guided by intuition alone and let go of the need to control. It seemed so simple yet, in many ways, I felt those innate capabilities were suppressed, ignored, or relegated to some kind of mystic hogwash. *How can we feel when our minds are a laptop with twenty-seven tabs open at any time of the day?* But there is truth to these abilities. 'Trust your gut,' 'Listen to your heart' – these phrases hold deep truths about what we are capable of as human beings. And the more I tapped in, the more I silenced that noise in my mind, the more life started to look different. I discovered abilities I had forgotten.

The bus finally made headway through the honking gauntlet of Kathmandu and we soon arrived at our destination. Pashupatinath Temple is one of the holiest sites in Nepal. Situated on the banks of the sacred Bagmati river (Nepal's equivalent to India's Ganges), the site is a confluence where life meets death. Daily cremations are held in venerated ceremonies on the funeral pyres erected along the banks of the river, as loved ones, and the occasional spying tourist, watch as the waning body, adorned with handmade leis of orange marigolds, transmutes into a mass of snowlike ash.

It seemed the more acquainted I became with myself, the more I acknowledged my own impermanence and, in turn, death. In the culture I grew up in, death is somewhat of a taboo topic. You know the day will come but it is never spoken about or ventilated unless someone close to you passes away, or an illness or ailment awakens you to the reality that the skin you wear is on borrowed time. I used to fear death, but a deeper reflection unveiled that it wasn't death itself I feared. It was a fear of loss, a fear of letting go of what I had and held in this lifetime and, perhaps, a small fear of the pain I may or may not endure in the moments leading up to my last breath of exquisite air. I was fortunate in the sense that death hadn't come up too much in my life. The closest person to me to ever pass over was my dear nan. I was only twenty-one when she passed. I knew nothing about death and a fragment more about life. I loved her though. I loved her so much and painfully felt her absence when she left. In some cosmic way, I still feel her. When I look down at the tattered gold ring on the middle finger of my left hand – her wedding ring, passed down to my mother and then to me – I feel her matriarchal presence. And sometimes, when I am deep in meditation or a pool of all-consuming emotions, I feel an angelic presence around me – an ancestral quilt of love and protection, just like the coloured blanket nan crocheted and wrapped me in as a child. On days like that, the veil between these two worlds doesn't feel so wide.

It's a hard pill to swallow when someone we love is no longer physically with us. It can be the cause of some of the deepest suffering known to humankind. Yet, paradoxically, we will all pass. There will come a time when every single person we have ever known is no longer here, and thus lies the great mystery of death; a mystery that strikes a different chord in each and every one of our lives, influenced by the doctrine we adhere to, the belief systems we hold or the sociocultural structures we are born into. What remains enduring is that none of us know what happens after we die, no matter how much we proclaim otherwise.

A silver smog concealed the sky above us as we walked down the road that led to the main centre of the temple grounds. Makeshift stalls lined the entrance, selling a range of products from marigold offerings to brass ornaments, to touristy trinkets like hemp bags and harem pants. For a significantly holy place, the grounds were unkempt. Pieces of discarded trash littered the sides of the road. As we approached a clearing, I noticed more trash beneath stone stupas carved with sculptures of Hindu Gods and deities smeared with the red markings of tika blessings. In the distance, above the shallow murky waters of a polluted Bagmati riverbed, I saw clouds of grey-white smoke emitting from burning flames. I didn't expect to be so close to the deeply sacred ceremonies, to witness death right before my eyes. I stopped, turning to look at Helge who was walking by my side.

"I'm not sure I feel comfortable enough to go over there," I said to him, confronted by the scenes before me.

"That's OK," he said, benevolently. "Let's walk to another part of the temple."

Helge was no stranger to death. He was a nurse who had spent time in end-of-life care and was deeply passionate about tending to people in the last days of their lives. He once told me about a book he read called *The Top Five Regrets Of The Dying*, by Bronnie Ware. The book was inspired by Bronnie's time as a palliative carer and the discussions she had with her patients about the regrets they had in life, or anything they would have done differently. Her discussions unveiled five common themes:

I wish I'd had the courage to live a life true to myself, not the life others expected of me.

I wish I hadn't worked so hard.

I wish I'd had the courage to express my feelings.

I wish I had stayed in touch with my friends.

I wish that I had let myself be happier.

I reflected on the findings he shared with me. I wouldn't have been ready to hear those words years beforehand when I actively lived a life contrary to my truest self. Perhaps in order to know who we are, we must first know who we are not. I believe our unique paths lead us to revelations when we are ready to hear them, when we are ready to acknowledge them. That's the beauty of free will, our innate ability to perceive the situations around us and make calculated decisions that shift our direction to wherever it is we ought to be going.

Maybe, in its dualistic nature, death helps to remind us to live fully, to love fully. Just like the rain reminds us that the sun will shine, and the night reminds us that the morning will come. I hope that we haven't forgotten the very miracle it is to be alive: to breathe, to witness a world full of endless possibilities. To be sure, this life isn't always rainbows, but it doesn't change the feeling that when the time of death approaches us, we are reminded of how much we have to live for.

That evening back at the hostel, as I lay on the bottom bunk of my dorm bed staring up at the wooden slats that supported the mattress above me, I thought more about impermanence. A few days earlier, I'd fittingly turned to a podcast by spiritual psychologist, Tara Brach, on the topic of grief, to help explain the sadness I held. She talked about the sentient being's perception of separation; how, ultimately, our fear of separation is what causes the pain and insecurity that stems from what we perceive as loss. In the podcast, she shared one of her routine anecdotal citations that tend to personify the sage wisdom of her talks. One quote she referenced from writer and philosopher Rainer Maria Rilke said:

> *Everything you love is very likely to be lost, but in the end, love will return in a different way.*

To come to terms with impermanence is to come to terms with loss, and to come to terms with loss is to come to terms with love. Grief is, ultimately, love transformed; a reminder that our souls are capable of feeling the most magnificent sentiment possibly existing on our emotional spectrum. To live is to feel it all. To be human is to exist in a world of insoluble polarities.

I closed my eyes as a tear fell over my cheek and down the right side of my face. I was finally starting to understand, to see this life in all its colours. Something shifted in me in Nepal. There was an awakening of sorts. I felt as if I were a child again with a whole new world of knowledge and perspective appearing before my eyes. I never thought I was searching for something when I made the decision to go to Nepal, but perhaps there were lessons to be had. As the saying goes, 'When the student is ready, the teacher will appear.' She called to me, the mighty Himalayas, just like lands call to us, to lead us along our destined paths. I can hear it now, the inner voice – that inner compass that shows us the way. I was ready to listen to it, even if that meant letting go of who I once was and of the life I once lived and embracing the next phase of my life. But letting go required mastery, and although Nepal aided in my evolution, much of me was still a young padawan.

Chapter 22 - A balsamic moon

The end of my volunteer placement with Local Women's Handicrafts was soon approaching and I was once again at a fork in the road of life, that junction we approach where we are asked to make a decision: the left turn or the right turn. The initial intention was to return to Australia when the placement had finished, but I could have never predicted the profound impact Nepal was going to have on me. It made me second guess going back and slipping quietly into the life I left – that square hole. I'd faced those crossroads before. They felt remarkably familiar. If that familiar fork in the road was marked with two signs, one would have read *The Unknown* and the other would have read *The Comfortable Familiar Place*. There was a magnetic pull to the unknown, it was a place formidable, yet limitless. The comfort zone, however, was safe; the trails were marked with dotted lines and gleaming street lights. It felt rather impetuous to extend my time in Nepal, to steer my wheel towards the right, but the thought, and the feeling, did enter my sphere of contemplation.

I once wrote a blog post titled, 'Travelling – why the best plan is no plan'. I talked about an all-embracing spontaneity approach to travel – adopting a literal go-with-the-flow mentality and making up the journey as one went along. The post was inspired by one of my trips abroad to the USA when I had eight days to spend in California before my flight home to Australia. I was travelling alone and felt a subtle notion to arrive with an impromptu intent. Just book your hostel in San Francisco and then decide where to go next once you get there, I thought. That inner voice was soon accompanied by contradicting arguments: *But what if you ... don't find accommodation, don't have enough time, don't meet any people...* and the list went on. So, I planned my travels to a tee and, lo and behold, within the first hours of arriving at the hostel, I connected deeply with some travellers who invited me on a precisely eight-day road trip from San Francisco to Los Angeles. Subsequently, I had to decline the offer to adhere to the plans I made which I had financially committed to.

Whenever I met a crossroads, I often reflected back on that example. Though, I wholeheartedly acknowledged there was an immense amount of trust required to adopt that kind of approach to life. It wasn't so easy to lean forward without hesitation, to look fear right in the face and say, 'You don't belong here.' And instead, trust your intuition or divine intervention.

One evening, in the days before my scheduled return flight to Australia, Raluca, Helge and I decided to treat ourselves to an above-backpacker-standard meal at the New Orleans Café, one of the more touristy eateries in Thamel. The hip hangout on Mandala Street had a rustic interior decorated with dimly lit fairy lights that enhanced the intimate aesthetic of the appropriately named restaurant turned jazz bar by night. The house wine I ordered wasn't exactly a sangiovese but its sweet sherried flavour sufficed. I relished the way the palliating comfort warmed my chest as I took a sip from the rounded glass. Helge sat opposite me, his long unkempt beard a symbol of his trodden miles, the clear quartz pendant on the black string around his neck a symbol of a connection to Earth. Raluca sat beside me. She was a beautiful young woman with eyes the colour of the sky after a storm. She had a septum piercing with a feminine brass hoop that matched her necklace and earrings. Her light ash brown hair draped to one side, flowing like waves.

"It feels strange to leave this place," I said to my friends as I twiddled the stem of the wine glass. "Being here has felt like a dream I don't want to wake up from."

"I understand how you feel," said Raluca.

I continued projecting my internal uncertainty into the safe space between us all.

"A part of me isn't sure about getting on that flight. I've grown so much, and I want to keep moving forward on this journey of growth. If I return to Australia, am I just taking a step backwards?"

"I don't think we ever go backwards in life," she replied. "You will never lose what you found in Nepal; it will always be a part of you. And now you can carry it, further on your journey to Australia and wherever you roam after that."

Her wisdom subdued my uncertainty like sand on a burning flame. I remembered the time I returned from Southeast Asia feeling a sense of defeat. But that was, too, growth. Although two years had passed since that journey, those memories and experiences had remained an evergreen part of my story. Maybe we don't ever go backwards. Just like the seedling that grows into the tree, maybe our sole purpose is to continue growing, collecting lessons and memories like lifelong tattoos inked into our skin. Perhaps growth is what we are here to embrace.

I eventually did return to Australia and spent the rest of 2017 back in the place that offered me not only familiarity but loving comfort too. I'd spent over thirty years of my life creating stories there – countless memories that could fill a thousand books. It was a place where the people I loved more than words greeted me with open arms no matter how far I'd roamed or how long I'd been away. Being back reminded me that love transcended time and space, and when I hugged my younger sisters, Christina and Alishia, for the first time in months, or when I sat with my childhood friends, Danielle and Ashleigh, laughing and reminiscing on our abiding, irreverent shenanigans, it made time seem fluid and illusionary.

In true Sydney style, it wasn't too long before I was swept up in the tide of routine and structure like a green sea turtle riding the East Australian Current. I'd moved into a run-down, yet homely, studio apartment situated in the leafy suburb of Neutral Bay. I increased my days back in the office to afford the rent for that apartment and attempted to reintegrate into society, jostling back inside the metaphorical marketplace, clinging tightly to the lessons and wisdom Nepal had gifted me.

It was the day of my niece Sienna's first birthday. I had been back in Sydney for a few months and while on the surface I seemed like the same girl I was when I left for Nepal, beneath that facade was a disoriented, despondent version of me wondering how to integrate the immense, intrinsic changes I had gone through. Despite being around my extended family for a day of celebration, I felt alone inside.

I remember that day so vividly: Sienna's adorable pink tulle tutu that matched the rectangular icing cake with hundreds and thousands decorated around the edges. A big pink balloon in the shape of the number one was tied to a string that stood taller than my Uncle Luc and swayed with the light winds. We can tend to remember the days of celebratory significance, but more so how we feel on those days. I remember that day so distinctly because something else happened.

"Are you OK?" Christina said as I took a sip of prosecco from my champagne glass.

"Sure," I said, curious as to what prompted the question. "Why do you ask?"

"I saw Dean's Instagram," she said, her serious face juxtaposing the joyful energy of the day.

My heart sank. I didn't have to probe the comment. I knew that behind the home screen of my mobile phone, on the digital grid that constituted the new-age equivalent of a collection of photographic fridge magnets, there was an image that would wound my heart and trigger impairing sadness.

When it came to romantic love, there was a difference between closing the door and leaving it unlocked and closing the door and throwing away the key. It solidified the end of the possibility and could bring grief right back to the surface as if you were reliving those last moments for the first time. Had I not already been struggling with my reintegration, perhaps, I'd have had the capacity to stand up tall and strong and shrug the whole thing off. I was happy for him, I truly was. He deserved to be happy and to be with someone who envisioned the same life path as him. But I wasn't strong in those months. I was weaker than I conveyed. And just like the straw that broke the camel's back, I broke.

Like the waxing moon phases, the tidal patterns of the ocean and the sacred feminine cycles of the womb, our lives are also subject to ebbs and flows. In those months following the news that the next season of my love story manuscript was cancelled, I sat beneath a sombre balsamic moon. During that time, I entered some of my most challenging emotional states. Although I was still functioning, the personification of hopelessness followed me – to work, to the grocery store. Hopelessness lay beside me in my bed as I cried myself to sleep most nights. He accompanied me to family gatherings, sat on the couch and watched *When Harry Met Sally* and *City of Angels* on repeat with me. I didn't tell many people about him. The thought of letting out our little secret felt too much to handle. After a while, I became used to him being around all the time. Some days, he was loud and obnoxious. On other days, he simply kept himself occupied, quietly, in a corner of my mind. Some days, specifically when the early October sun coated Sydney with warmth, he would surprise me by motivating me to get out of bed, walk to St Leonard's Park and find a grassy patch to sit between scattered trees and feel the sunshine on my face.

What guided me in those challenging times were the lessons I learned in Nepal. What my time in Nepal helped me understand was that – contrary to the Western school of thought that implied pharmaceuticals and escapism would solve my problems – acceptance, self-compassion and mindfulness were my true paths to refuge. To be human is to exist in a world of insoluble polarities, I reminded myself as the golden sunlight radiated through my closed eyes. I thought about the impermanence of that blissful moment and, inversely, the impermanence of the sadness I was feeling. I thought about Jai and our serendipitous meeting in the café. Maybe the lesson sadness was teaching me was simply to accept and trust that I was exactly where I was supposed to be at that moment. I'd been through a lot of changes that year. It was only human to require the time and space I needed to heal, to truly heal.

Healing can be painful. But healing is growth, and growth is an opportunity – a chance to integrate the lessons we learn in this school of life and to unlearn some of the conscious and unconscious habits we've formed that no longer serve us. Through my own personal hardships, through my own sadness that had emerged from my experiences with separation and detachment, I had been gifted an opportunity to reflect on how I could approach these with more self-compassion and understanding. To not mask my open wounds with distraction or escapism and instead sit with the feelings that had arisen and investigate them, be with them and ask them what they were revealing to me.

So, I sat on that grass beneath a glistening sun and closed my eyes. I took a deep breath in and softly whispered to myself,

May I be patient.

May I be present.

May I trust.

And then I breathed out slowly, exhaling carbon dioxide like I was whooshing out the emotions that passed through me. When I opened my eyes, the colours of the foliage looked a mildly brighter shade of green. I was reminded of the ever-changing patterns of life, the constant flow of energy shapeshifting like the spume of the waves at Bondi Beach. And the gift of our own perception: to witness that transformation, both in us and around us.

I stood up, bent over to pick up the floral cardigan-turned picnic blanket and brushed off the blades of grass that stuck to it. Hopelessness got up too. Like me, he was sun-kissed.

"Tomorrow's a new day," I said to him. "Let's see where it takes us."

Chapter 23 - The Wish game

As Earth continued its 365-day orbit around the sun and the fiery autumn leaves rained on Sydney, I found myself, one very impromptu Thursday evening, standing at a white picket gate that led down a pebbled pathway to the front door of a seaside house in Sydney's northern suburb of Fairlight. My friend, Kathy, had invited me to a game night led by one of her close acquaintances, Karen.

Kathy and I were introduced by a mutual friend who witnessed our shared values surrounding kindness and equality. After years of public advocacy, I'd developed somewhat of a philanthropic stereotype for myself: 'You'd have a lot to talk about with Bianca, she wants to change the world too,' were the words that initiated many of my professional connections in the succeeding years when I shook away the last remnants of my identity as a corporate executive. If I was lucky, those connections would evolve into more than professional relationships. And I was lucky with Kathy. We complemented each other like yin and yang. At the time, Kathy ran a social enterprise selling vibrant-coloured flip-flops engraved with value words like 'grateful', 'peace' and 'freedom'. For every pair of flip-flops sold, funds would be donated to support educational projects in rural India. Simultaneously, I had started a venture with a similar business model: selling recycled sari kaftans made by the women at Local Women's Handicrafts, with the aim to distribute profits back to Nasreen and her cause. Although it felt good to be able to offer some kind of assistance to the women after my return from Nepal, running that small business wasn't an easy feat. It involved waking up at six am most weekends to set up tables and gazebos at markets across Sydney and then standing around all day in rain, hail or shine in the hope that the products would be chosen among the surfeit of other vendors who had also woken at the crack of dawn to assemble their enticing displays. I felt like one of those green three-eyed alien toys in *Toy Story*'s Space Crane waiting to be picked by The Claw. Except, for me, The Claw was simply enough money to cover the cost of the market stall for the day, and then maybe enough to cover the net cost of the goods, and then, hopefully, step away with some funds to send back to the women in Nepal. Not to mention the reimbursement for my time, which was usually only ever paid to me in the currency of benevolence. Albeit my landlord didn't accept benevolence as an exchange for renting the apartment.

At least, those mornings standing on the corner of a pedestrian thoroughfare at Orange Grove Markets, I had Kathy with me. We learned a lot about each other in those months. We became each other's sounding boards – an encouraging mirrored reflection of our inner workings. We were both endlessly curious and unconventional free spirits, humanly and spiritually designed to move through this life with purpose. And we ungrudgingly held space for one another. I was grateful for that.

I realised in the earlier years of my life, I'd often placed a lot of exclusive value on my romantic relationships, as if they stood on a pedestal above all others. But as I grew older, I started to deeply acknowledge the way love manifested in my life outside the romanticised cliché of the coupled dynamic. I felt I had become a little brainwashed by the media's aggrandising of romance in television, movies and songs, that it somewhat blinded me from recognising the countless other manifestations of love, and receiving them, like the deep inhalation of the air you breathe when you emerge from the shallows of the ocean. Perhaps I watched *Crazy Beautiful* too many times as a rebellious teenager and convinced myself I was Kirsten Dunst, about to be saved by the handsome Jay Hernandez and whisked off into the sunset.

I'll admit, I walked through life with rose-coloured glasses, but I couldn't help but wonder, had I become so fixated on the glorified idea of "the one" that it stole my attention away from all the other magnificent facets of love? *Perhaps finding one blanket definition for*

a word that is infinite is as complex as solving the 'E = mc2' equivalent for global equality?
Nevertheless, I realised the more I opened my heart to receive love in areas outside of romance, the more nourishing my life became.

Kathy and I entered the Fairlight home and were escorted to the dining room. We were joined by six other women, all there to participate in an evening of manifestation. We sat at a round table, neatly decorated with a centrepiece of lilies that had been pushed aside to make room for the lapis-coloured game board.

"Has anyone ever played *The Wish* game before?" Karen said, acting as our generous host for the evening.

"Not me," said one of the women. "Neither I," said another.

I shook my head, curiously staring down at the board centred with a figure-eight design and patterned with symbols like butterflies, keys and the tree of life. Atop the board was a deck of cards, similar to those in the game of *Monopoly*, and eight gemstones.

"*The Wish* is an energy game that helps us to manifest our greatest wishes," Karen said. "The aim is to come up with a detailed wish and then, throughout the game, help each other more clearly define that wish and unravel what it is we truly desire. We will also help each other uncover the energetic blocks that are getting in the way of attaining our wishes, whether that be limiting beliefs, imposter syndrome or something else," she continued.

As Karen was speaking, I was reminded of the metaphysical concept of manifestation. It is a topic so prevalent in popular psychology and renowned by admired influential teachers like Ekhart Tolle, Joe Dispenza and Gabrielle Bernstein. A popular read among the people I met on my travels was *The Alchemist* by Paul Coelho. I had a paperback copy tucked away in a box somewhere among the cluster of a lifetimes' worth of belongings that still collected dust from the built-in wardrobes of my father's home. I always remember one profound quote from that book:

And, when you want something, all the universe conspires in helping you to achieve it.

"I'll give you all ten minutes to write down your wish. Be specific. Think tangibly. Feel into what it is you truly want and when you want it by." Karen guided us through the rules of the game. Within seconds after her directions, all of us had pen-to-paper.

"What do I want?" is an interesting question to ask ourselves. We are a nexus of complexities with subjective needs that are constantly changing, depending on where we are in our lives. A common response may be to want money or to win the lottery. I would have a jar full of money if I deposited a coin every time my friends or family members said, "When I win the lottery I will ... take the holiday, buy the home, do the thing I've always wanted to do ..." and so on. Indeed, money makes it easier to navigate the chessboard of this economic game, but money is only a tool we use to take us to where we wish to be – to fill in what we feel we lack. So, then the question may become, what do I wish for to feel whole? To feel as though my intrinsic human needs are being met: to be seen, to be heard, to be loved, to wake up every day and know I am on the path I am meant to be on. It's easy to perceive that what we lack comes from outside of us, that money or fame or fortune will ultimately make us happy in the long term. But the more I unravelled this mystery of life, the more I felt what we perceive we lack comes from within us: our own unalignment; the pain we aren't able to heal yet; the courage we've lost; the self-love that lies stagnant beneath an overgrowth of societal conditioning, others' expectations, perpetual judgement and deep-rooted suppression that disallows us from unapologetically shining our individuality into this world.

I stared down at the paper in front of me. *What did I wish for?* The past years had offered me so many opportunities to grow, to explore this world, to meet myself in ways I never could before. I felt like I had already gained so much. *Was I even deserving of the opportunity to ask for more?*

I'd struggled with imposter syndrome for longer than I dared to admit to myself: limiting beliefs that fed me thoughts like I wasn't deserving of greatness, that I shouldn't overshadow anyone else with my successes or that I wasn't good enough to shine. I was getting tired of those beliefs. They pulled me down and kept me small. And they were untrue. We are *all* deserving of greatness, including me.

So it was there in that room, among an inspiring collective of feminine energy, that I gently placed another wish out into the universe. I wished for something that would change the course of my life and once again guide my soul in the direction it ought to be going. I looked down at the written manifestation; it was now in the form of neatly handwritten swirls of blank ink.

I wish to become location independent and to access the flexible living circumstances that will offer me the time and mental space to share my message across multiple mediums, including interviews and a published book, so I can divinely inspire others to live their truth. I wish to help them connect with themselves and with one another and ultimately, make a positive impact in the world.

Step one was complete. My wish was out there like the prayers of a child on Christmas eve. Now came the real work – believing I was deserving of that wish and that I could attain it. Believing it so deeply, as though it had already happened, and I was looking back on the envisioned wish I'd lived out in its true form.

I folded the piece of paper and placed it between the back of my mobile phone and the rubber phone case. I intended for it to be near me but not to open it and re-read it until the year came to an end. Joe Dispenza speaks about the element of letting go when it comes to manifestation – detaching from the timeframe and outcome and embracing radical trust. Trusting that you are the dancer and life is the dance.   Letting   go   is   the   key.

Chapter 24 - Soul truth

I turned thirty-two that year, surrounded by my closest friends at a hipster, graffitied corner pub in Sydney's inner-west. I'd only thought about the wish a few times since that evening in Fairlight. The swells of schedules and responsibilities occupied the space in my mind and *The Wish* game eventually subdued into a whirlpool of faded memories. Still, the piece of paper hid, stagnantly, beneath my atlas-printed phone case that rarely left my side.

Soon after my birthday, I'd taken a recurring trip to northern New South Wales for the July extravaganza that was Splendour In The Grass. The annual festival is one of Australia's biggest music events, occurring each year on the last weekend in July. I had been attending the festival routinely for nine consecutive years (except for that one year I spent abroad) alongside a group of close friends who'd become my Splendour family. The tradition became our yearly rendezvous – a time to retreat into the hills of the North Byron Parklands, paint ourselves in body glitter and dance like nobody was watching.

Punters from all across the country made their way to the four-day dance-fest, packing their cars with camping gear, Doc Martens and alcoholic beverages that were cleverly hidden in every possible nook and cranny of their vehicles. As security at the festival tightened over the years, so did the innovative ways people invented to smuggle the now prohibited BYO substances into the festival: liquid storage packs sealed and stuffed into pillow cases, bottles hidden inside loaves of Wonder White bread, watermelons infused with vodka. It was uncanny what festivalgoers would do to expedite a good time. And Splendour In The Grass was the cream-of-the-crop when it came to a good time. It was an atmosphere where you felt uninhibited – free to sing, dance and be whoever you wanted to be. I admired that about music festivals like Splendour, Glastonbury and Burning Man. They were a magnet for the untethered – a place to feel truly liberated.

We'd pitched our tents and tarpaulins ready for a weekend of conscious debauchery. There wasn't a cloud in the sky as the mild winter sun peered down on the striped purple and white picnic rug that lay nearby our Jucy campervan. I lay down on my back with my face to the sun like a lizard baking on a rock in the ochre outback. My friend, Kate, joined me.

"How have you been feeling lately?" Kate said as she turned her face towards mine. The sparkle of her glittered face jewels shone in the midday sun. "I know last year was tough for you. You seem to be doing much better."

I lifted one hand to shield the rays from my eyes and turned to face Kate.

"I'm doing much better," I responded. "I've been feeling like I'm ready to take the next steps in my journey. I feel the pull to leave Australia again."

"I can sense that," Kate said. "You're such a global citizen these days, I feel like you could feel too confined here."

"In some ways, I do," I replied. "Of course, I will always have a sense of home here but the desire to leave is strong. When I came back from Nepal last year, I wasn't ready to let go – of my identity here, of Dean – but I think I'm ready now. It's hard to change course in life, especially when our old identities are so cemented in everything around us."

Kate continued to listen to my heart's song. The bass of the first live band's music, blaring through speakers, hummed in the far distance.

"Just the other day, my friend, and also mentor, asked me to reflect on the phrase, 'I am ninety … what do I want to think when I look back on my life?' and it really got me thinking about where I am headed and what I really want. I think about Nepal often, and my journeys abroad – how much they shaped me. I think about where I've had my most profound revelations, the places and situations that have helped me grow. I looked back at my life through the eyes of the older version of me and I saw a woman with courage – a woman who moved through life driven by intuition, purpose and passion."

"I see that for you, Schmee," Kate said, referring to me by the nickname we'd created for each other one intoxicated Splendour evening. "Your intuition is strong. Keep following it. I support you no matter what."

"Thank you," I said sincerely as I looked into her eyes and smiled. We hadn't seen each other in almost a year but no matter how much time passed, Kate always felt like sunshine in human form to me.

Spring was a spectacular season. Especially, in Australia, as wildflowers awakened and native animals like wombats, platypuses and echidnas birthed their young. Spring always reminded me of the ever-flowing nature of this life. Change was inevitable. No matter how much we resisted or clung to sameness, what once was, would not always be.

In many ways, the reality of our variable nature could complement the way we lived our lives, depending on how we perceived that reality. Did the tree perceive its leaves falling as a loss, or as a transformation? Either way, it was inevitable that the leaves would fall, that change would take place and that spring would return again.

When the time came for me to decide on how I would embrace the next chapters in my life, I thought about the tree and the seasons – the ability to let go of what once was and embrace what would emerge like seeds that fell to the ground and sprouted anew. In the months leading up to October 2018, the messages from my soul had been getting louder. Subconsciously, I had started to imagine what my life would look like if the wish I projected that evening, surrounded by the power of manifestation, came true. Although I wished to become location independent so I could share my messages with the world, I feel as though what I really longed for was the courage to walk the next steps of this journey on my own, without the safety nets I depended so strongly on. I wanted to steer my ship down an estuary to the open sea and live deeply aligned with my values.

I evaluated my life from its current vantage point. I had less money than I'd had in the previous ten years. I had fewer belongings. I had my career and roads that led to Sydney's sandy beaches. I was happy. But if the meaning of life was to be happy, then seasons wouldn't change and storms wouldn't come. Flowers wouldn't wither and our bodies wouldn't wane.

The meaning of life was much more than happiness. If I'd learned anything from those past years when I'd stood on the border between who I once was and who I was to become, as the ground shook beneath me, it was to shift my compass from my head to my heart. I wasn't chasing happiness anymore – I was simply dismantling the walls erected around me that inhibited me from accessing the wisdom required to flow with the natural rhythms of the universe, to hear the voices that whispered around me and within me, guiding me along the way.

I couldn't help but feel I had already arrived here with a purpose – that I wasn't searching for it but merely lifting the veil so I could see it, so I could feel it. Perhaps we all have an inclination of our soul's true purpose: what it was we are really here for. But the fortresses around us and that we build within us are so tall that we've lost sight of the way. When we come face to face with our truth, unchained, maybe only then can we discover the meaning of freedom. And if we don't meet our truth, or can't, our inner congruence will continue to shake, like the tectonic plates of the earth, shifting until we find our balance.

On the day I stood beneath the office building on Alexander Street, as the smell of roasted coffee beans from the cafe greeted my senses, I looked up at the glass-paned windows that reflected the morning blue sky. I'd learned, by then, how to separate my inner truth from the noise that surrounded it, like finding a diamond submerged in kimberlite. To know oneself was to trust oneself, and that day I trusted my decision to state my desire to pivot to a full-time remote position in the company. I was no longer the anxious girl that paced up and down the footpath terrified of asking for what I wanted, of writing this life's story in my own words.

I'd spent so long behind walls, adhering to others' expectations of me, following rules and regulations that confined me and prevented me from living in alignment. I even erected some of those bricks myself; I believed I wasn't capable of stepping into the infinite power that emanated from my being like the spirit of a star. I conformed, I settled, and I got so lost inside the maze of my comfort zone that I could barely find my way out. But I did find my way – we all do eventually – because I loved myself enough to believe it was possible.

And in the end, that's the most love we can give ourselves – to allow ourselves to walk this life in a trusting presence, guided by our soul truth.

Notes

Chapter 5: Descending the corporate ladder

Jim Carrey at MIU: Commencement address at the 2014 graduation -

https://www.youtube.com/watch?v=V80-gPkpH6M

Chapter 6: A sacrifice

The talk that inspired my blog name - Peter Singer: The why and how of effective altruism -

https://www.youtube.com/watch?v=Diuv3XZQXyc

The Altruistic Traveller blog –

https://thealtruistictraveller.com/

The Hero's Journey was first referenced in this book -

The Hero with a Thousand Faces (The Collected Works of Joseph Campbell).

Chapter 9: Borders

CouchSurfing - the hospitality exchange service -

https://www.couchsurfing.com/

Referencing the historic treatment of asylum seekers in Australia –

Ethics and Exclusion: Representations of Sovereignty in Australia's Approach to Asylum-Seekers by Katharine Gelber and Matt McDonald.

https://www.jstor.org/stable/40072138

Referencing sustainable tourism –

https://thealtruistictraveller.com/what-is-responsible-tourism/

Chapter 10 – Banana pancakes

The destination website for Chi Phat, Cambodia –

http://chi-phat.org/

The Mondulkiri Project elephant sanctuary-

https://www.mondulkiriproject.org/

Recommended book about the Khmer Rouge –

First They Killed My Father by Luong Ung.

Chapter 11 – Sliding doors

Socially-minded eateries in Siem Reap, Cambodia –

https://thealtruistictraveller.com/blog/food-good-ethical-eateries-siem-reap/

Phare Circus, Siem Reap, Cambodia –

https://pharecircus.org/

Recommended book about ancient structures and their alignment with the sun –

Fingerprints of the Gods: The Evidence of Earth's Lost Civilization by Graham Hancock.

Chapter 13 – Farm to table

Organisations working to remove unexploded ordinances from Laos and Vietnam –

The Mines Advisory Group

https://www.maginternational.org/

APOPO Hero Rats

https://apopo.org/

Mr Khamsone's coffee venture and guided tours –

http://www.mysticmountain.coffee/

Referencing fair trade coffee and its international governance –

https://www.fairtrade.net/product/coffee

Chapter 14 – 7000 islands

About the World Wildlife Fund's whale shark conservation in Donsol, Philippines –

https://wwf.org.ph/resource-center/story-archives-2019/whale-shark-commitment-renewal/

The articles I wrote for the World Fair Trade Organisation (WFTO) –

https://wfto-asia.com/2016/06/11/land-is-life-farmers-fight-for-justice-in-the-philippines/

https://wfto-asia.com/2016/06/11/fair-trade-helps-women-rebuild-their-lives/

Chapter 15: Golden eras

Book reference –

Burmese Days by George Orwell.

The Yangon walking tour –

https://www.freeyangonwalks.com/

Learn more about Irrawaddy dolphin conservation in Burma –

https://burmadolphins.com/project/

JoAnna Haugen's storytelling platform at the intersection of sustainable travel, environmental conservation, and community-based advocacy efforts –

https://rootedstorytelling.com/

Chapter 18: A Himalayan calling

Workaway – the homestays and cultural exchange platform -

https://www.workaway.info/

Nasreen's fair trade store and anti-slavery platform –

https://localwomenshandicrafts.com/

https://empowermentcollective.org/

Chapter 19: Kathmandu

A resource about the global campaign against fast fashion –

https://www.fashionrevolution.org/

Organisations working in sustainable community development in Nepal –

Clean City

https://www.cleancity.global/

Conscious Impact

https://www.consciousimpact.org/

Chapter 21: Awakening

Book reference –

The Top Five Regrets Of The Dying by Bronnie Ware

The quote from Rainer Maria Rilke is from his book, *Letters to a Young Poet.* The quote appears in Letter 8.

Find Tara Brach's podcasts, meditations and teachings on her website –

https://www.tarabrach.com/

Chapter 23: The Wish game

The Wish game can be found at the below link –

https://www.thewish8.com/we-wish

Recommended books about manifestation –

The Universe Has Your Back by Gabrielle Bernstein

The Alchemist by Paulo Coelho

Becoming Supernatural by Joe Dispenza

The Power Of Now by Eckhart Tolle

Acknowledgments

There hasn't been a moment that has gone by on this journey when I haven't felt supported by the people around me. I have been truly blessed in this life to have received gifts in human form. Writing this book was no easy feat. But this whole journey, this whole life – even as I write these words – wouldn't be the same without the people I love and the people who have loved me back. You have made my life what it is. You are, and will always be, a part of this story.

I want to especially thank my two beautiful sisters, Christina and Alishia, for being there for me on this journey. I love you both so much. To my Auntie Leanne, thank you for believing in me, for inspiring me and for sending me your constant words of encouragement. Thank you, Mum, for supporting me and for picking up the phone a thousand times over, listening to my heart's song. To Dad, Auntie Frances, Uncle Luc, Auntie Doris and Janet, thank you for watching over me on this journey, even when I may have made those spontaneous, impromptu decisions that made your heart skip a beat.

To my incredible circle of soul sisters, Ana, Steph, Danielle, Ashleigh, Kate, Bonney, Amy, Amber, Christine, Michelle, Kathy, Jarka, Sarah, Ellie, Tiff, Claire C, Claire T, Linn, Ness, Mandeep, Mandy and the rest of you incredible women, thank you for being a beacon of light in my life and for constantly supporting me no matter how great the geographical distance is between us. To my soul brothers, Light, Jonathan, Dean G, Rich, Ryan, Helge, Tarek and the rest, thank you for your strength and love.

Thank you to Nigel and the team in the office for being my backbone as I took the time away to write this book in my motherland of Malta. I am truly grateful for the way you constantly support me and the unconventional way I choose to live my life.

To Conor, thank you for being a part of this story and for the beautiful memories we created together all those years ago. And to Dean, the star of my show. You played such a hand in the creation of this story, of this book. Thank you for allowing me a place in your heart and for loving me unconditionally all these years. I wouldn't be where I am today if I hadn't met you.

To my editor, Heather, to my cover designer, Valentina, and to all my friends and family who offered their time, thank you for helping me polish the book and get it ready for the world to see.

I'd like to also specially thank the other people who played a strong role in my life during the timeline of this story: all the people I met on my travels, those who offered me a roof over my head, those who fed me, those who accompanied me on long journeys across the continent and those who shared their story with me.

It's been an absolute honour to share the stories of the people who dedicate their lives to making our world better. I only hope that their story, that our story, can inspire others to make a positive impact on the world around us and shape our future for the better.

And lastly, thank you, dear reader, for coming along on this journey with us.

You are magic. Never believe anything otherwise.

Love and light,

~ B

Printed in Great Britain
by Amazon

24802452R00138